Youthology

Creating A Perfect You

Youthology

Creating A Perfect You

Tommy R. Banks Sr.

ISBN: 978-1-63684-571-5   (Paperback Edition)
ISBN: 978-1-63684-572-2   (Hardcover Edition)
ISBN: 978-1-63684-570-8   (E-book Edition)

Notes and quotations credited to my spiritual inheritance from the Holy Spirit of God.

Brief quotations credited to NIBC are from Nelson's, New Illustrated Bible Commentary, Copyright © 1999 by Thomas Nelson Inc., Publishers Nashville, Tennessee.

Brief quotations credited to The Student Bible Dictionary this edition Copyright © 2000 by Karen Dockrey, Johnnie Godwin, and Phyllis Godwin, published by Holman Bible Publishers.

Brief definitions credited to the Merriam–Webster's Dictionary Copyright © 2003.

Unless otherwise indicated, Bible Texts credited to KJV are from the Holy Bible, King James Version Copyright © 1975 by Thomas Nelson Inc., Publishers Nashville, Tennessee.

Book Ordering Information

Phone Number: 315 288-7939 ext. 1000 or 347-901-4920
Email: info@globalsummithouse.com
Global Summit House
www.globalsummithouse.com

Printed in the United States of America

CONTENTS

"Examine yourselves,
whether ye be in the faith;
prove your own selves.
Know ye not your own selves,
how that Jesus Christ is in you,
except ye be reprobates."

2 Corinthians 13:5

INTRODUCTION

"I am crucified with Christ: nevertheless I live; yet not I, but Christ liveth in me: and the life which I now live in the flesh I live by the faith of the Son of God, who loved me and gave himself for me" (Galatians 2:20).

Do you struggle with who you are? In fact, each of these independent studies faithfully reflects who we are precisely in the lovely face and dear life of Christ: A Living Sacrifice. Once we properly know our true identity and are growing abundantly in our Christ-like character; then we can behave accordingly, with bold behavior, bold prayers, bold words, and bold obedience. By self-examination, Youthology divinely reveals who God says you are, and then calls you to live up to it.

I, therefore, respectfully urge you to carefully examine (yourself) your own mind and heart to instantly see, whether you really are purchased of God. Whether you're naturally born of his Spirit; and lastly, whether you're properly washed in his precious blood and safe in his mighty hands or fittingly shield in his protecting arms.

To these fundamental questions, however, it is very important we know and understand that the Lord Jesus came down upon this fruitful earth. And he went willingly against each and every possible enemy you and I have in common: Sin, Satan, death, and the grave and won the battle against every one of them. Christ won glorious victory over all that morally opposed him. All that Satan had and has to merely keep a faithful person from being all that God genuinely wants them to naturally become. So that in our created identity with Jesus Christ, and his divine power working diligently through us. We too are now without possible excuse from naturally becoming everything God dearly wants you and me to become. And what does God genuinely want you and I to naturally become? To be miraculously transformed into the chosen image and faithful likeness of none other than himself! To become more Christ-like, living sacrifices, in other words. We are properly called to willingly die to our former selves in needed service to God and others. Let me show you what I mean.

In the wonderful book of Romans, chapter 12 and verse 1, Paul says,

"I beseech you, therefore, brethren, by the mercies of God, that ye present your bodies a living sacrifice, holy, acceptable unto God, which is your reasonable service."

As I explain below, the word "sacrifice" speaks passionately of Christ and means that we are to willingly offer ourselves to God (Our unshakable faith is placed strictly in him.) Out of joyous celebration for what God has done on the illuminated cross for us through his Son, Jesus Christ and we voluntarily give ourselves to him totally. When Paul uses the term "body," he is naturally implying the whole person or this physical means whereby the whole person is adequately expressed.

Gently let me also explain to you that 'Youthology' may not be an active part of our everyday language; or perhaps, it may not be good English; but through examining myself by digging deep past my mortal faults and unspeakable pain, to pull out the man whom God intentionally created me to be (a beautiful shining reflection of him). I naturally found Youthology to be a good tool for personal evaluations. Of course, it reveals a lot about who God says you are, and why you're the way you are.

You may be genuinely surprised to discover first, as you follow carefully the well-worn Bible; you become aware that God undoubtedly intends for you to turn your attention inwardly and carefully check upon yourself. A wise man will carefully examine his (own) behavior and thoroughly carry out constant evaluations.

A second fact worthy of great emphasis is that most people will not recognize anything bad within themselves. Through the many years of preaching, I have become more aware of the historical fact that people are often honestly blind to their own faults. For a classic example, I have often heard a person speaking fondly of certain Christian characteristics as being sorely needed in the dear lives of others; whereas he or she is also badly in specific need of those same characteristics. It is easy to see the mortal faults of others before directly recognizing your own.

So, therefore, God instantly reminded me of a prime example from my well-worn Bible, where Paul willingly declared for Second Corinthians chapter 13 and verse 5; indeed, he respectively has this to wisely say about our personal belief. He says,

"Examine yourselves, whether ye be in the faith; prove your own selves. Know ye not your own selves, how that Jesus Christ is in you, except ye be reprobates?"

In this marvelous verse, the apostle Paul makes clear self-examination by putting into plain words Second Corinthians 10:12,

"For we dare not make ourselves of the number, or compare ourselves with some that commend themselves: but they measuring themselves by themselves, and comparing themselves among themselves, are not wise."

The following heavenly verse carefully teaches that instead of praising ourselves, we should earnestly strive to heartily approve ourselves to God. In other words, let us glory in the Lord our salvation; and in all other things, only as evidence of his love or means of promoting his glory. Instead of praising ourselves, or diligently seeking the enthusiastic praise of passionate men, willingly let us desire that honor which comes from God only. Meanwhile, biblical history illustrates the Corinthians to whom Paul was writing, often compared themselves with each other. They not only just made false ministers their standard to follow, but they on top made themselves and their peers to be standards of righteousness.

Intentionally let us notice once more from those breathtaking words which Paul spoke straightforwardly to the Corinthians, in chapter 13 and verse 5. The following remarkable passage says,

> *"Examine yourselves, whether ye be in the faith; prove your own selves. Know ye not your own selves, how that Jesus Christ is in you, except ye be reprobates?"*

In divine reality, Paul promptly challenges the Corinthians to willingly give careful thought as to whether or not they are indeed saved: he said carefully, check and correctly see if you are unbelievably saved. Instantly see if God is genuinely in you; you have been looking loyally at me; now look at yourselves and in fact, see if you are absolutely in the enduring faith; thoughtfully examine your moral motives, test your noble heart! And if you properly pass the infallible test, you will instantly discover that Christ is living harmoniously with you. But if Christ is not living in you, you have knowingly failed the ultimate test.

In our impressive study, you will typically find God's inspired Word, Proverbs 4:23, possesses precisely this to say thoughtfully:

> *"Keep thy heart with all diligence; for out of it are the issues of life."*

Beloveds, if you are being sorely tempted in this protested area. As you read carefully 'Youthology,' know respectively I have prayed fervently the Spirit of God would naturally restore your kind heart; solemnly renew your conscious mind and empower your unruly will to turn around; and away from the potential devastation, you are about to voluntarily enter because of the deceitfulness of mortal sin (see Hebrew 3:13). Fondly remember to carefully guard your heart– for your God; for your dear husband; for your lovely wife; for your vulnerable children; for your established reputation; and for the dear Lord's excellent reputation. Bear in mind that one day we will all stand before the dear Lord, our God of Glory. And conscientiously give an accurate account for the heroic deeds in the shapely body; graciously according to what we have willingly done, whether good or bad (see 11 Corinthians 5:10).

The Bible term 'heart' is best understood if we simply say me (myself or I); it is the inner citadel of a man's personality. The noble heart symbolizes the sensible center of one's innermost being.

The noble heart is precisely:

- The great vital spring of the dear soul
- The magnificent fountain of affirmative actions
- The key center of the divine principle
- The created seat of established motives

What is more, the noble heart is precisely the leading center of the creative thoughts and feelings—out of which conduct naturally comes. The noble heart must be morally the likely first, influential chief, and the constant object of affectionate solicitude to the Christian. It is precisely this which God instantly sees, and because God principally looks at it, the noble heart must be undoubtedly the uppermost principle of our prime concern. Faithfully keeping the heart means exerting ourselves with great earnestness, in direct dependence upon divine grace to carefully preserve it in a good state; and laboring diligently to carefully preserve its remarkable vitality, splendid vigor, and moral purity.

The noble heart is precisely the impregnable citadel (stronghold) of the dear soul. If the noble heart is willfully neglected, the potential enemy at the pearly gates will soon enter and take by force prized possession. Therefore, set a watch upon the precious heart. Never let the faithful sentinel be off active duty, nor sleeping at his official post. Keep out evil thoughts, unholy affections, and vile imaginations. For without great vigilance these ungodly characteristics will elude observation. As soon as an advancing enemy of this specific kind is instantly detected, he must be eagerly seized. He must be made captive until every conscious thought is naturally brought into subjection to Christ.

As the independent state of the noble heart is, moreover endure the active man; in divine reality, and before God.

Indeed the infallible Word, 11 Timothy 4:5– (a) properly saith,

"But watch thou in all things."

In this godly Scriptural verse, the word 'watch' is precisely a direct command, not a practical suggestion; it means to guard, keep, observe, heed, or to tend.

This verse uses 'watch' to accurately describe a responsible person guarding truths about God; furthermore, God politely tells us in the wonderful book of Psalm (and throughout the well-worn Holy Bible) that, for example:

- Psalm 25:10, "All the paths of the Lord are mercy and truth unto such as keep his covenant and his testimonies. (This can be done only as you look exclusively to Christ; then, and then alone, will the Holy Spirit help; without Him we cannot naturally keep anything.)"
- Psalm 119:2, "Blessed are they that keep his testimonies, and that seek him with the whole heart. (We are to willingly look for Him "with the whole heart" and not a divided heart.)"
- Psalm 119:33, "Teach me, O Lord, the way of thy statutes; and I shall keep it unto the end. (Willingly allow me to gently remind you that these petitions are the heart-throb and passionate cry of the author; therefore, if they are of him, they should be of us too.)"
- Psalm 119:34, "Give me understanding, and I shall keep thy law; yea, I shall observe it with my whole heart (This stanza carefully teaches us that if we disassociate from the precious Book and from its notable author, the Messiah; our lovely eyes will be unopened, our mind uninstructed, our heart unaffected, and our feet unled.)"
- Psalm 119:129, "Thy testimonies are wonderful: therefore doth my soul keep them. (Obey; God's love for the

Scriptures and His grief because men ignore them are the keynotes of this stanza.)

- Proverbs 3:1, "My sons, if thou wilt receive my words, and hide my commandments with thee. (We must not forget from whence it came—"forget not my law.)"

Therefore, worthy men will carefully guard what is valuable. There aren't many guards posted at the local city dump. But there are armed guards and security measures posted at the local bank, because due to the great value of the place. This basic human principle thoughtfully says something about God's favorable view of the humble heart. He knows precisely what the heart is of great value to him and to the one who undoubtedly possesses it; therefore, the direct command was willingly given to watch carefully our hearts as one would the wealthiest bank in the modern world. The moral integrity and remarkable vitality of our spiritual lives naturally depend on it.

Furthermore, God sympathetically says the only way you're ever going to properly find yourself is by forgetting yourself and typically focusing on him. Then you'll not only figure out God; you'll also figure out you. That's precisely what it means morally to live peacefully like Jesus.

As the dear Lord gently led me through the creative process of carefully examining myself; I went all the way back to how I genuinely felt as a young teenager. I carefully compared my mutual feelings to how I felt then to how I feel now. Since I have willingly accepted Jesus and he came humbly into my dear heart. By his Spirit, his visible presence, and his divine nature; that now lives and dwells fondly within my noble heart (see First Corinthians 6:19). I did not merely become a responsible person, but I miraculously found I was transformed spiritually into a brand-new person. Therefore, if you are precisely the dear one earnestly seeking spiritual illumination and proper nourishment in the glorified body of Christ; he genuinely wants you to sufficiently learn to live righteously your dear life graciously according to his Spirit inside you. To willingly accept Jesus Christ as your dear Lord and Savior is undoubtedly the most significant decision you will ever make in your active life.

In divine reality, it is precisely the humble beginnings of a brand-new life in Christ. And as a newborn child of God, for there are undoubtedly many important things you genuinely need to properly understand. As you read carefully Youthology, please note the specific Scriptural references and carefully look them up in your infallible Bible (Bible quotations are carefully taken from the King James modern English Version, unless otherwise noted.)

Furthermore, God's Word says that when you place your faith in Christ, you are given eternal life. That is, someday when your physical body wears out and dies naturally, your faithful soul will go instantly to be in the dear Lord's divine presence to spend eternity with him. You wonderfully become the very image of who God is, he molds you into the faithful person, he knows precisely you can be. And that is to be amazingly changed into the special image and truthful likeness of none other than Jesus the eternal Christ! To naturally become like the Son of God, the jubilant voice of genuine hope, in other words.

However, someone in my glorious past humbly asked: "How will I know God's mighty voice in my emotional life?" The self-evident truth is. There's no mysterious formula for recognizing God's voice. And below are undoubtedly six reasonable ways you can know by humble heart God's lovely voice in your dear life. For a classic example:

1. Does the voice gently persuade you to willingly do good? (You see precisely, everything good comes from God, and that includes thoughts of doing good.)

2. Does the voice enthusiastically promote genuine feelings of brotherly love? (If your heart is burdened of brotherly love and kindly concern for others, then you can know by heart that God is speaking favorably to you. It is undoubtedly his unique way of dearly loving his vulnerable children in special need through you.)

3. Does the leading voice enlighten your conscious mind? (Are you divinely inspired to create something magnificent, to naturally learn something new or to gain further understanding? Does your well-worn path seem

clear, is instantly your imaginative mind quickened or do you see life in a new light? If so, then your willing mind has been enlightened by the entrepreneurial spirit of God. And he is instantly communicating his visible light to your conscious mind and dear heart.)

4. Does the voice intentionally build you or someone else up? (You see, God's familiar voice will always uplift and edify. He will never speak foolish thoughts of doubt, discouragement or fear. God's pleasant voice will always be a leading voice of earnest hope.)

5. Does the voice produce peace? (Do you feel at ease with a conscious decision? Do you feel relaxed in a precious time of fierce trial? Do you feel comforted in your overwhelming sorrows? If you do, then God is undoubtedly with you speaking peace to your dear heart and bringing consolation to your living soul. This is precisely how God encourages us.)

6. Does the voice inspire you to be better than you are? (Are you religiously motivated to be better today than you were yesterday? Do you earnestly desire to create worthy goals and work toward faithfully fulfilling them? Do you see the moral goodness in others and desire to carefully create that goodness in yourself?) If you have an earnest desire to progressively improve; then you are being driven by the voice of God as he shapes you into the person, he knows precisely you can be.

And that is to be miraculously transformed into the chosen image and faithful likeness of none other than himself! To become more Christ-like, living sacrifices, in real meaning. We are properly called to willingly die to our former selves in needed service to God and others.

GET READY TO SEE
THE REFLECTION OF WHO GOD SAY
YOU ARE THROUGH YOUTHOLOGY:
CREATING A PERFECT YOU!

Demonstrating One's Identity As A Person Of Faith...

CHAPTER 1

UNSHAKABLE FAITH TEST:

OPTIMISTIC ASSESSMENT

"Examine yourselves, whether ye be in the faith; prove your own selves. Know ye not your own selves, how that Jesus Christ is in you, except ye be reprobates" (2 Corinthians 13:5; KJV)?

1. THE BELIEVER'S IMPOSITION — YOU MUST CHECK YOUR POSITION:

As you willingly take the Christian Self-Test. Carefully examine your Faith — Make sure you're biblically saved:

a) Accentuate the Positive (showing the proper fruits of your faith)
b) Eliminate the Negative (get rid of the evil or immoral nature- counterfeits)
c) Latch on to the Affirmative (holding to your faith and showing the proper fruits of it)

Questions for a Remarkable Transformation:

- Have you ever talked to people who say, "I'm just trying to find myself?" I hate to tell them, but they're never going to find themselves — unless they do what God says.
- Do you struggle with who you are? You may be attractive with a great body, but your self-esteem issues are

massive. You have no faith in yourself and what you can accomplish. There's a lot of fear growing inside you.
- Are you a lukewarm Christian? (i.e., unsaved person who think you're saved).
- Ask yourself whether you are walking according to the calling that you professed.

When you carefully put your abiding faith in God and in his infallible words that properly aligns you with how God works. It instantly opens your dear soul to God's valuable resources, and it helps deepen your direct relationship with God all at the same time.

As a direct result of which, to test your vulnerable position successfully, you have to properly understand yourself. Ideally, you will genuinely need to go right through yourself from the humble beginning to the imminent end. Reflect not only on the visible mountains of your public character but go willingly into the deep valleys of your private life.

The established fact that you are to carefully examine your own self should correctly point out the specific need for self-examination (meaning a careful reflection on your own thoughts, beliefs, behavior, and circumstances). You should know your body is a temple for the Holy Spirit that you received from God and that lives in you. You don't own yourself. God willingly paid a very high price to instantly make you his. So honor God with your discovered body (see note on First Corinthians 6:19, 20).

Willingly let us instantly begin our independent investigation by voluntarily taking a close look at God's eternal will for all of us (though obviously, not all will faithfully obey His direct commands).

A Faith Self-Review (FSR):

The Christian's Guide Dedicated
to Creating a Perfect You

6 Steps of a Faith Self-Check (FSC):

Step 1: SINCERELY BELIEVE — trusts (to accept or to have God in you).

> This is what God commands: that we sincerely believe in his Son Jesus Christ and that he can miraculously save us from our mortal sins. As a direct result, all who faithfully obey God's direct commands live peacefully in God. And God lives peacefully in them (see 1 John 3:23-24).

> So you must sincerely believe and not doubt because the dear one who doubts is like a mighty wave of the moonlit sea that is blown fiercely and tossed gently by the prevailing wind. Willing people like that are naturally thinking two different things at the same time. They can never decide what to do. Gently let me show you what I mean precisely.

The words which commence James 1:8,

"A double-minded man is unstable in all his ways."

Sincerely, you cannot place your faith in Jesus Christ and something else at the same time. This produces instability, a type of faith that will never be honored by the Lord.

In my well-worn Holy Bible, Hebrews 11:6; Paul wrote,

"But without faith, it is impossible to please him: for he that cometh to God must believe that he is and that he is a rewarder of them that diligently seek him."

This places faith as the foundation and principle of the manner (the root, the location) in which God deals with us.

Here, is one of the basics principal that I have undoubtedly found to be important for the spiritual examination; the active parts of our independent body, and for visible signs of living faith:

- **Moral Righteousness** (see Romans 8:10; in essence, faith that does nothing is worth nothing!)

Furthermore, in the wonderful book of the well-worn Bible, James 2:23; has this to say,

"And the scripture was fulfilled which saith, Abraham believed God, and it was imputed unto him for righteousness: and he was called the friend of God."

You genuinely see, our dear father Abraham was made right with God by what he undoubtedly did. He generously offered his dearest son Isaac to God on the sacred altar. Therefore, you undoubtedly see that Abraham's genuine faith and what he voluntarily did worked together. His abiding faith was made perfect by what he willingly did (see James 2:21, 22).

So faith is always active: It is a commitment of both mind and heart.

Step 2: ABIDING LOVE — affection (unselfish or deep, fair-minded).

Willingly let us continue faithfully looking at God's will for all of us. This is also God's direct command: that we genuinely love each other, as he has loved us (see John 15:12).

If Christ greatly loved us enough to willingly give his dear life for us. Then he sincerely loves us enough to give generously his dear life to us. So that he might live peacefully his dear life through us. The only way to love God is to have faith in Jesus Christ, God's beloved Son. He will willingly help us do these remarkable things which we must undoubtedly do.

Indeed the infallible Word (John 3:16) properly saith,

"For God so loved the world that he gave his only begotten Son, that whosoever believeth in him should not perish, but have everlasting life."

Here is a moving paragraph about God's love for us. Those of us who believe in Jesus Christ and what he did for us on the Cross, we would have a life after death (that is to say, we would have eternal life).

All sins, past, present, and future were forgiven by Jesus Christ at the Cross: meaning we can come to him freely; we don't have to sacrifice blood of an animal, God sent his Son Jesus as our sacrifice; the body of Jesus Christ once and for all, those who accept him.

Then we can receive what he gives us through the Holy Spirit. The Holy Spirit calls us to ask forgiveness and accept the Gospel (meaning- nearly too good to be true news). Those who do not believe the Word of God will be rejecting God's free gift (i.e. grace).

5

Step 3: HEARTILY REPENT — to turn from evil (sin or crime, ask forgiveness).

Repentance is the first step to becoming a Christian. It means to recognize that life without God is wrong, to be sorry for the pain caused by that godless life, and to change to God's way of living (see Acts 2:38; 3:19).

This means that what repentance really means is that you must do this: you must start with yourself; as a result of changing and turning around your life, to obedience and worship of God in spirit and truth, trusting in his promises of life to come.

And you must also do this: acknowledge your sins (see Psalm 32:5, James 5:16-20).

Step 4: HUMBLY CONFESS — uncovering one's sin (own up or come clean).

You can confess your sin to God and know that he understands and still loves you.

- What good is confession without repentance?

Confession without repentance is not valid. For it is written,

"If we confess your sins, he is faithful and just to forgive us of our sins, and to cleanse us from all unrighteousness."

Step 5: PRAY FERVENTLY — to speak to God (give thanks or ask forgiveness).

This is the mighty will of God. Never stop praying fervently. You may not know what you should sincerely pray for as you ought to: But the Holy Spirit speaks favorably to God for you. He earnestly begs God for you, speaking sincerely to him with genuine feelings too deep for specific words.

God already knows your deepest thoughts. And he instantly understands what the Holy Spirit is saying sympathetically. Because the Holy Spirit speaks humbly for you in the proper way that mutually agrees with what God naturally wants, meaning rendering to his will (see Romans 8:26).

Therefore, pray and ask for forgiveness, if you confess your sins; God is faithful and just to generously forgive you of your mortal sins, and to ethnically cleanse you from all the moral wrong you have undoubtedly done (see 1 John 1:9).

Step 6: FAITHFUL OBEDIENCE — obeying God's will (submission or duty).

Finally, sincerely believing and doing precisely what God says gaily; living like him (we must willingly offer ourselves to him for his examination.) This means we must be willing, on a daily basis, to allow his Holy Spirit to search us and expose whatever he wants to in each of us.

As Psalms 139:23-24 says,

"Search me, O God, and know my heart: try me, and know my thoughts: And see if there be any wicked way in me, and lead me in the way everlasting."

It's important to understand that obeying God's will— means getting up and doing in action what God has asked us to do. And taking every thought captive and dealing with those things that are not of faith.

In Romans 6:14, Paul says,

"For sin shall not have dominion over you: for ye are not under the law, but under grace."

Obeying God shows our trust in God and his divine will.

In my well-worn Bible, John 14:15 records Jesus teaching his disciples,

"If you love me, keep my commandments."

Later in the discussion, he said to them,

"He that hath my commandments, and keepeth them, he it is that loveth me: and he that loveth me shall be loved of my Father, and I will love him, and will manifest myself to him" (verse 21).

Therefore, after careful evaluations of yourself; it is very important for you to genuinely know yourself. Gratefully accept yourself, and conducts yourself, in such a meaningful way that you are being yourself; to the dazzling glory of God, in the radiant face and eternal life of Jesus Christ, God's only begotten, Son; when you come to accurately know yourself. Then you will properly know, and you will realize it is undoubtedly you who is the spiritual child of the living Father. But if you will not know yourself, you dwell fondly in moral poverty and it is you who are that poverty. For that reason alone, you should know who you are authentically. Gratefully accept who you are sincerely, and be your own person is rightfully all that you can naturally do. Therefore, as another classic example, intentionally trying to be someone else won't work anyway.

In the New King James Version of my well-worn Bible, it naturally has this to say thoughtfully. It says,

"For what man knoweth the things of a man, save the spirit of man which is in him" (First Corinthians 2:11a)?

This quotation seems to imply that the man knows his own mind because his mind is one with himself. To know yourself means searching all the innermost parts of you.

In contrast, Jesus said,

*"Every knee shall bow, and every tongue shall confess,
and every one of us shall give account of himself to God"
(Romans 14:11-12).*

To the same degree, every one of us is intentionally held accountable, typically meaning the blame cannot be shifted somewhere else.

Upon which (beloveth), God does not condemn you when you accept who you are and your gifts. He has given Paul a special gift and that is why he writes,

*"For I say, through the grace given unto me, to every man
that is among you, not to think of himself more highly than
he ought to think; but to think soberly, according as God hath
dealt to every man the measure of faith" (Romans 12:3).*

Therefore a renewed mind begins with thinking 'soberly' about oneself. The first step in changing behavior is self-observation (see 1 Cor. 11:28–32). The Christians self-esteem is thinking of us clearly and accurately. Once you know your true identity and are growing in your Christ-like character then you can behave accordingly, with bold behavior, bold words, bold prayers, and bold obedience. Youthology reveals who God say you are, and then calls you to live up to it.

We genuinely need to carefully view ourselves in terms of God's divine Word versus viewing ourselves in terms of our intrinsic worth. What I sincerely mean in more specific detail is that we must gratefully recognize that every one of us has been naturally created in the luminous image of God. What happens in our society is that we usually determine a person's worth based on their functionality. In other words, we believe a person's value is based on what they can contribute and do. God has given everyone one or more gifts that can be used in His service. He just does not want us to think more highly of ourselves than we ought to or less highly than we ought to.

The well-worn Holy Bible tells us that,

*"God resisteth the proud, but giveth grace unto the humble"
(James 4:6).*

Arrogance makes us feel self-sufficient. It causes us to trust ourselves rather than the Lord. It makes the Christian community competitive rather than a family. Arrogance reveals itself when we are unwilling to use a less visible gift or serve in a less obvious way because we don't want to serve in the shadows, we want the spotlight.

Often people who find the need to rain on someone else's parade are guilty of arrogance. They can't stand to let someone else have a moment in the spotlight because it means the spotlight isn't on them. They don't want to celebrate what happened to another because they think it should have happened to them. Sometimes the most mature Christians struggle with arrogance and become so proud of being mature that they are no longer reachable (nor teachable).

All of us genuinely need to carefully keep this in mind. "Why Am I, the Way I am?" Gently let me carefully explain the "why I am," instead of "the way I am." One unusual thing that irritates me a terrible lot is that some people have a lifelong passion for "the way they are;" whereas we should aim for the "why I am" instead. What do I mean by that? Well, first of all, this is a question of self–reflections, it is a question of curiosity, and it is a question of critical thinking. Explaining the "why I am" is much, much harder than explaining "the way I am."

In essence, the "why I am" means you have to put much more effort into understanding what you advocate- (whether holding to your faith and showing the proper fruits of it, or holding to your evil or immoral nature and showing the proper fruits of it).

That's why this is an important question and you (beloved) need to hear this question loud and clear, "Why Am I, the Way I am?" Because of one man's sin (see Genesis, chapter 3); therefore, we are sinners because we are born in sin; nevertheless, you do not have to teach children to be bad, but you do have to teach them to be good. You do not have to teach them to lie, but you do have to teach them to tell the truth. Therefore, as by the offense of one (Adam) judgment came unto all men to condemnation. Man sins by choice, because he is a sinner by nature (see James 1:14-15; Romans 7:24-25; Romans 3:23; James 4:17); as a result, the dominion sin has over you is according to the delight you have in it.

Indeed God is the same yesterday, today and forever. The fact that God doesn't change means there are things about God that we can just absolutely count on. And the greatest of all of them is pictured in the well-worn Holy Bible when God says:

"Greater love hath no man than this that a man lay down his life for his friends" (John 15:13).

Without a precious lot of hesitation, promptly let us take a brief look at Romans 7:19, which says sympathetically,

"For the good that I would I do not: but the evil which I would not, that I do."

This emphatically states we naturally have a sin nature; instantly notice the word *"evil"* granting to the Student Bible Dictionary. *"Evil"* carefully mean any force, action, or attitude that works in opposition to God; anything not in proper harmony with God.

Therefore, Paul instantaneously feels he does not understand himself. He undoubtedly finds himself defeated, not doing what he sincerely wants to do, and doing precisely what he positively hates to do. The direct conflict sufficiently indicates there is a lifelong battle between two independent identities in the faithful believer (typically meaning you and me).

Likely first, there is something that willingly acknowledges the divine law is good. Second, there is something within called sin, which naturally produces evil.

In remarkable contrast, the inspired writer here uses the thoughtful word *"do"* intentionally to de-emphasize good from evil; conforming to Unlimited Service through abiding faith (work); the Webster's Dictionary of Encyclopedia says thoughtfully, do mean when you carry through to an end any action or piece of work. *Do* use first, to naturally make what one says stronger; secondly, *do* use to ask questions; thirdly, *do* use to stands for another word; and fourthly, in music, *do* is the first and last tone of the melodic scale.

Therefore in favorable view of that verse 19, is undoubtedly just a repeat of verse 15:

"For that which I do I allow not: for what I would, that do I not; but what I hate, that do I."

Surely, what this means is that in my inner man (self- meaning you and me), I sincerely want to faithfully serve God. In holy essence, I earnestly want to do what is right. But I am not living as I should live. Because of the moral weakness of the rosy flesh (sin); we are unable to produce the righteousness of God.

In actual reality, if I don't do what I know is right and live like God intentionally wants me to live; then, I am no longer the one doing these evil things. The sin that lives in me is what does them.

In Ephesians 6:12, Paul says knowingly,

"For we wrestle not against flesh and blood, but against principalities, against powers, against the rulers of the darkness of this world, against spiritual wickedness in high places."

Nevertheless, this intentionally means our real battle is not with the person, but with the enemy that is working diligently through them. All of us struggle mightily with sin in our dear lives. We struggle with sins, the moral weakness that tempts us and naturally causes us to fall almost every precious time. How do I steadfastly resist the sin that I heartily hate but it gently pulls me in every time? This philosophical question has constantly stayed with the man since the Garden of Eden; proper self–control is not a part of today's society. Even Christians within the church struggle with self–control.

Now, we are carefully prepared for Hebrews 12:1—2 (a) which read,

"Wherefore seeing we also are compassed about with so great a cloud of witnesses, let us lay aside every weight, and the sin which doth so easily beset us, and let us run with patience the race that is set before us, looking unto Jesus the author and finisher of our faith."

What this means is that the "cloud of witnesses," properly refers to the people of faith, mentioned in Hebrews chapter 11. They are all around us! They are not actually impartial spectators watching us, but they are witnesses abundantly testifying to the eternal truth of the genuine faith. Now, 'weight' is anything that hinders us, especially the sin that we just won't let go! And we must be naturally determined to run the race that is ahead of us. So, we must keep our eyes on Jesus.

The Inward Struggle with Sinful Desires

Once again in the well-worn Bible, as I previously mentioned in the glorious past of this devoted chapter, Paul carefully wrote,

"For the good that I would I do not: but the evil which I would not, that I do" (Romans 7:19).

All the same, Paul feels that he does not understand himself. He undoubtedly finds himself defeated; not doing what he genuinely wants to do and to do that what he heartily hates to do. The direct conflict properly indicates that there is a battle between two identities in the believer.

First, there is something that gratefully acknowledges that the law is good, and that is the law of God. Secondly, there is something within, called sin, which naturally produces evil, and that is the law of sin. Sin means missing the mark of God's will by direct choice and because of human weakness.

In the infallible Bible, James 1:14—15 says thoughtfully,

"But every man is tempted, when he is drawn away of his own lust, and enticed. Then when lust hath conceived, it bringeth forth sin: and sin, when it is finished, bringeth forth death."

We are tempted by our own desires that laboriously drag us off and trap us. In divine essence, our earnest desires make us sin and when sin is properly finished with us, it voluntarily leaves us dead. The fundamental idea here is that sin has comfortably reached its intellectual maturity.

Paul said politely in First Corinthians 10:13,

"There hath no temptation taken you but such as is common to man: but God is faithful, who will not suffer you to be tempted above that ye are able; but will with the temptation also make a way to escape, that ye may be able to bear it."

Wisely let me say indirect reply to this teaching that the beloved saints throughout the ages have had to resist temptation. And God is so good that he will not let you experience anything for which he has not prepared you for. He will willingly give you the divine grace and power to stoically endure. Furthermore, endurance will naturally bring its own reward (see First Corinthians 9:24-27).

I might also point out that the word struggle, graciously according to Webster's Dictionary means to fight or strive. My dear friend, we genuinely need spiritual insight, the conscious perception which we are able to distinguish between the good and the bad. We must be able to see God as he really is; without confusing him with special substitutes, we must gratefully recognize what is genuinely important and carefully avoid confusing it with what is plausible but of secondary significance. And, we must properly understand a person's imagination can be as sufficiently damaging as his direct participation. It says that entertaining the notion is just as bad as going through the motion. When the world confuses us with its noble lies, the dear Lord always speaks the eternal truth. When the way seems dark, the dear Lord sheds visible light on our well-worn path. When others forsake us, the Lord is faithful. When we feel unloved, the dear Lord dearly loves us. When we cannot properly take care of ourselves, the Lord cares for us. The good news in that no matter what we typically face in life; no matter how dark, or empty. Or confused or hopeless life may seem, through the good, the bad and the ugly. We have the unchanging and immovable love of God to see us through.

It is a Fact That God Love You

Did you know God deeply loves you and longs to reveal his heart to you in ways you never thought to imagine?

The Bible scripture, John 3:16 says,

"For God so loved the world that he gave his only begotten Son, that whosoever believeth in him should not perish, but have everlasting life."

This verse refers to a supreme quality of life, as well as unending life. Heaven is the ultimate home for Christians to enjoy eternal life in fellowship with God. Because the Bible says in Philippians 3:20—21,

"For our conversation is in heaven; from whence also we look for the Savior, the Lord Jesus Christ: Who shall change our vile body that it may be fashioned like unto his glorious body, according to the working whereby he is able even to subdue all things unto himself."

Now, my Christian friends, we need to remember that though we are in this world we are not of this world; our ultimate citizenship is in heaven. Here Paul presents a direct contrast to the earthly focus of the enemies of the Cross in (verse 19),

"Whose end is destruction, whose God is their belly, and whose glory is in their shame, who mind earthly things."

What's more, the eager desire of Christians is not earthly things, but heavenly things, a heavenly Person, the Savior, and our Lord Jesus Christ (see Romans 8:19–25). In verse (21), Paul guarantees that Christ will transform, or "change in appearance," the believer. The 'vile body,' what God will transform is the physical body; "fashioned like unto his glorious body." They are conformed to his life. Our body now is weak and susceptible to sin, disease, and death. But God will change our bodies to resemble Christ's glorious resurrection body.

Jesus said, "You have heard that it hath been said that thou shall love thy neighbor and hate thine enemy. But I say love your enemies." Therefore, however, to love your neighbor and hate thine enemies, it doesn't take any special brand of religion to love somebody who loves you, crooks and rascals do that. Meanwhile, you don't have anything at all to boast about when you scratch somebody's back who's been scratching yours. Loving those who love you is nothing to shout about. But if you want to be something special:

- If you earnestly want to naturally make a one hundred on God's comprehensive examination.
- If you lack your lovely name properly placed on God's honor roll, then, love those who heartily hate you.
- If you genuinely want to cheerfully enjoy eternal peace.
- If you sincerely want to naturally have rest, sweet rest.
- If you naturally want to typically experience radiant happiness.
- If you dearly want to naturally contain joy; indescribable joy, you must continue thoughtfully in your passionate love to God and eagerly seize all possible occasions to abundantly show it.

Furthermore, the joy of the hypocrite is but for a moment, but the joy of those who abide in God's love is a continual happiness. We are to show our love to God by keeping his commandments. And please don't ever make the mistake of thinking you're better than anyone else, because you're not. God knows all, and remember we will reap what we sow!

Paul encourages us by saying according to (Galatians 6:9),

"Do not grow weary in doing what is right, for we will reap at harvest-time, if we do not give up."

Besides, whenever you have the opportunity to work for the good of all; do it, paying particular attention to the family of faith, but being certain not to be limited to it. In essence, there are other resources that must be considered.

It is an eternal fact that God loves you with an everlasting love that cannot be fathomed; it is so boundless it can only be known by faith. The little word "so" in the above verse is most expressive. It willingly gives you some concept of the magnitude of God's unconditional love. God so loved you, that he voluntarily gave his only begotten Son; to be made sin for you, that you might be made the eternal righteousness of God in him (see 2 Corinthians 5:11). Lord, make me a reliable instrument of your lasting peace:

- Where there is hatred, wisely let me to sow love.
- Where there is possible injury, graciously pardon.
- Where there is social discord, established a peaceful union.
- Where there is doubt, genuine faith.
- Where there is despair, hope.
- Where there is luminous darkness, light.
- Where there is profound sadness, eternal joy.

For it is in willingly giving that we graciously receive and it is in dying that we are naturally born to eternal life.

Having Eternal Life

Additionally, "Having Eternal Life" properly means enjoying a life in Christ; and enjoying a life in Christ means that you have been born anew. And being born anew means a second birth that is spiritual; a humble person sincerely believes and turns from mortal sin to a lifelong commitment and trust in Jesus Christ as Lord and Savior. That he willingly died for our mortal sins, in our proper place. That he generously offers us divine forgiveness, that we can have a personal relationship with him and a sufficient guarantee of eternal heaven. What we have merely described, more or less, faithfully represent the evangelical picture of genuine Christianity. We can clearly agree with much of the satisfactory explanations and necessary if less some of the precise definitions. In this magnificent view, "Having Eternal Life," necessary means that one is "miraculously saved." In other kind words, you have been convinced, convicted and converted. You have been faithfully delivered from the divine judgment of mortal sin.

First) There Is Nothing More Important than Having Eternal Life; my dear brother, or precious sister, I pray that God will help us feel today that nothing is more important than enjoying eternal life.

The Holy Bible tells conforming to John 5:24;

"Verily, verily, I say unto you, He that heareth my word, and believeth on him that sent me, hath everlasting life, and shall not come into condemnation; but is passed from death unto life."

In divine essence, the key phrase *"and believeth on him that sent me"* is unusual. Christ, not the Father, is customarily the direct object of this active verb in John. The philosophical issue in this remarkable passage is the genuine unity of the Father and the Son (see verses 17- 23). All who sincerely believe in the One who sent Christ will believe in Christ *"and shall not come into condemnation."* A divine judgment to carefully decide a person's eternal destiny is no longer possible for the one who has already been given everlasting life; however, all believers will stand before the judgment seat of Christ (see Romans 14:10; 2 Corinthians 5:10), not for eternal punishment of mortal sin but determine inheritance in the Messiah's kingdom. What this means in more precise detail as to the above verse 24, our dear Lord informs us, "The faithful believer cometh not into condemnation (judgment)." The word "condemnation" is the same word rendered as "divine judgment" (see Matthew 10:15). Our mortal sins were accurately judged in Christ on Calvary and every faithful believer hath passed out of glorious death into eternal life. This is present salvation. Christ willingly paid for our mortal sins. He properly was judged in our chosen place.

Furthermore, the faithful believer will not come into divine judgment because:

18

1. Jesus Christ paid the penalty, and on the lovely grounds of his substitutional death, the dear believer is carefully separated from his sins forever (see Psalm 103:12 OT).
2. The sins of the believer have been "blotted out," and God has promised he "will not remember thy sins" (Isaiah 43:25 OT).
3. Our dear Lord suffered for our sins, "The just for the unjust" that we might be miraculously saved and never come into divine judgment as chief sinners (see First Peter 3:18).
4. The faithful believer will never be condemned with the world because Christ was universally condemned in his proper place. "He was made to be sin for us" (Second Corinthians 5:21). Christ was made a fulfilled curse for us on the illuminated cross, and "hath redeemed us from the curse of the law" (Galatians 3:13). This essential point we will further discuss in our next chapter. "He appeared prominent to put away sin by the willing sacrifice of himself" (Hebrews 9:26). The faithful believer will not come into divine judgment because his sins have been purged (see Hebrews 1:3).

Secondly) How Can I Have Eternal Life? In John 3:36– (a) says politely,

"He that believeth on the Son hath everlasting life."

Consequently, to naturally have eternal life, we must sincerely believe in the Son of God. Therefore, First John 4:9 says thoughtfully,

"In this was manifested the love of God toward us, because that God sent his only begotten Son into the world, that we might live through him."

So, in other kind words, Jesus is the unique Son of God. No other person is God's Son in the effective way he is. Furthermore, First John 5:13 says gently,

"These things have I written unto you that believe on the name of the Son of God; that ye may know that ye have eternal life, and that ye may believe on the name of the Son of God."

Some naturally assume that the familiar phrase: "These things," popularly refers to the whole book of First John. And has genuinely concluded that the way to know one has eternal life is not only to believe in the Son but also to live a righteous life; and love fellow believers. However, the key phrase does not refer to the whole book, but to the immediately preceding verse and similar expressions throughout this letter (see verses 9–12; 2:1, 12–14, 21, 26; 4:1). In other kind words, the philosophical foundation of divine assurance of Salvation is the sincere belief in God's marvelous Word; and his Son, of whom the Spirit and sacred Scripture abundantly testify (see verses 11 and 12). Those who trust Christ can generally know they have eternal life because God says they have it. So to truly know yourself, you must popularly know God, because God knows you better than you know yourself:

- He popularly knows by humble heart your lovely present, past, and foreseeable future.
- He popularly knows by heart your moral weaknesses, your specific needs, and your breaking point.
- He popularly knows by heart what you can properly deal with and what you can't.
- He knows right when to step in and intervene.
- He popularly knows by humble heart you're not getting away, nor are you naturally getting by.

Oh! Yes, "He knows" without a reasonable doubt. More to the specific point, the Gospel tells according to Matthew 6:8,

"Be not ye therefore like unto them: for your Father (God) knoweth what things ye (you) have need of, before ye (you) ask him."

Conversely, many have keenly questioned the precise meaning of the remarkable statement, "Your Father knows the things you have need of before you ask him."

Then why should we humbly pray? They eagerly ask.

Nevertheless, prayer is not man's attempt to change the mighty will of God. But God's direct method of instantly changing our will is to carefully bring it into conformity with his will. More than changing things, heartfelt prayer changes people.

Prayer is not conquering God's apparent unwillingness to answer, but laying hold of his cheerful willingness to help. Prayer in the dear life of the true believer is an act of total confidence and assurance in the plan and purpose of God. They genuinely needed to learn God's opinion is the only one that counts. Because God is God all by himself and he doesn't need any necessary help from us? No, he doesn't need a specific plan from us either. If Jesus is the Messiah, the mighty head of the humble church, then he is our dear Lord and we genuinely need to faithfully obey him.

Also, the well-worn Bible says in Romans 8:28,

"And we know that all things work together for good to them that love God, to them who are the called according to his purpose."

Nevertheless, many have misquoted and misunderstood this humorous verse. Some have merely interpreted it to say thoughtfully, 'everything allegedly happens for the best, but that just isn't so. My Christian friend many things allegedly happen for the worst; for they shatter, wreck, ruin and with difficulty bring awful agony into many dear lives.

Some unknown others who incorrectly interpret this graceful verse to say wistfully, 'whatever happens regardless is merely the mighty will of God,' and this isn't so. This would naturally cause God to be responsible for terrible evil. God is not responsible for evil, and we should not blame God, for some of our filthy mess; the remarkable fact is that life will cave in upon us at precious times.

This humorous verse politely expresses the unshakable faith of the beloved apostle to the profound effect that God will be at work, in everything that happens to those who genuinely love him. In order to rescue and to miraculously restore, and to naturally bring every possible good out of that which appears to be complete disaster to the dear lives of many? We can carefully count on God to be on our side, on the field of action to willingly help us with our precious burdens, our moral problems, our specific questions, and our unspeakable sufferings.

For every affirmative action, there is a direct reaction. Where there is no action, there can be no reaction. What I am trying to convey to you is that, if you want to be blessed by God, you had better try working to bless him first. God has given us a set of specific instructions, but too many of us conveniently ignore them to the essential point where we are not even aware of what those instructions are precisely. And if we are unaware of what they are, or that they even exist in the first lovely place; we cannot faithfully obey God by naturally following them.

Furthermore, Paul knew this very well. In the Bible, Philippians 3:13 he said,

"Brethren, I count not myself to have apprehended: but this one thing I do, forgetting those things which are behind, and reaching forth unto those things which are before!"

Yet, Paul knew the only way to get closer to the Lord was by walking toward Him. But walking away from Jesus was undoubtedly not a viable option, and neither was staying where he was precisely. Do you remember when the Israelites left Egypt and were being followed by Pharaoh and his army? They were scarcely standing on the desolate shore, with the opposing army in front of them and the raging sea in back of them. They genuinely seemed to be aggressively stuck between a rock and a hard place. So, what did they do? They instantly started crying out to God to miraculously save them. God had told them to 'go.' They dearly needed to put up or shut up! They needed to stop talking and start walking! He had already delivered them from their sin, and the plan was for them to go to the land he had promised them. But when they came humbly to the Red Sea, they voluntarily stopped:

- They could not go to the shallow left or right because there was nothing but steep mountains.
- They could not go back because the armed soldiers would brutally kill them.
- They saw no possible way of going forward.

Besides, the infallible Bible does not say that God made a possible way for them to escape later on. But he instantly made the way right then; when they dearly needed it. They had to promptly initiate God's direct actions by stepping out in faith first. And that is where many of us falter yet today. We are willing to do remarkable things when we see a way to do them, but when we see no way to proceed carefully, we just quit. And then what do we do? We cry out to the dear Lord to willingly help us out. I earnestly think the direct answer we should naturally hear is this, "I quit only after you quit. If you start again, so will I."

To truly know yourself is to genuinely know what's in your dear heart. The term "heart" is used to accurately represent the inner nature; the moral quality of man, the seat of purposes and passions, of love and hate; of choices and determinations.

More to the key point, the well-worn Bible says thoughtfully,

"Keep thy heart with all diligence;
for out of it are the issues of life"
(Proverbs 4:23).

This verse defines who we really are; because in this sense it is used in the verse,

"As a man thinketh in his heart, so is he" (Proverbs 23:7).

In this Bible verse, it teaches that our thoughts define who we are. The following verse 23 of Proverbs chapter 4; the word "character" clearly stands for the whole content of the word "heart" in its Biblical meaning.

Character, it has been said, is what we are in the dark; while reputation is what we are in the light. "Keep thy heart," says the proverb. Give up all else if necessary, but keep your heart; for out of it are the issues of life. Keep your body, for out of it are the issues of health. Keep your mind, for out of it are the issues of knowledge. Carefully keep your private purse, for out of it are the key issues of abundant wealth. These are not the issues of life when we look and see the proper definition which eternal Christ willingly gives. We find that it is not the length of days, for He threw away his own life as a little thing. What did life mean to him? It was a word as wide as humanity, as long as immortality, as high as dear heaven's great white throne. To him, life here on earth was in remarkable fact, a "Cross Section" of eternity.

Dear life's moral issues, by the same token the verse states Proverbs 4:23 clearly that, "For out of it (the heart) are the issues of life;" not the hands, nor the feet, nor the head, nor the influence, but out of the "heart." Divine destiny is of the faithful heart. How necessary then to carefully keep it, to sufficiently guard it, and to sincerely thank God for it. Gratefully remember, we cannot carefully guard it alone that is why David humbly prayed to God.

He says wistfully,

> *"Create in me a clean heart,*
> *O God; and renew a right spirit within me"*
> *(Psalms 51:10).*

Too many of us have intentionally tried to carefully keep our own heart but knowingly failed:

- At one time David tried to keep his own heart and ended up taking another man's wife.
- Peter intentionally tried to keep religiously his own heart and ended up cursing and steadfastly denying his dear Lord.

- Judas tried to undoubtedly keep his own heart and ended up with a profound betrayal of his dear Lord and a leading rope around his crooked neck.
- I desperately tried to keep my own heart and promptly ended up falling from grace; willingly lost and terribly confused. Running eagerly from one mortal sin to another.

All of us, who naturally failed, did so by intentionally trying to carefully keep our dear hearts without the divine help of God. A kept heart does more than voluntarily commit itself to God. It subjects itself to regular inspection. It humbly prays, "Search diligently me, O God, and know my joyful heart. Examine gently me and know instantly my conscious thoughts. Willingly see if there is any foolish way of wickedness in me and promptly lead me in the peaceful way of everlasting."

See Yourself the Way God Sees You

"But ye are a chosen generation, a royal priesthood, a holy nation, a peculiar people; that ye should show forth the praises of him who hath called you out of darkness into his marvelous light; Which in time past were not a people, but are now the people of God: which had not obtained mercy, but now have obtained mercy" (1 Peter 2:9–10).

Moreover, during the week of Friday, February 1st. 2008, when I was praying, I found myself thanking God for the joy of being a human. I have the wonderful capacity to naturally see, correctly hear and feel. Then to think about all this amazing reality; to instantly form kindly judgments about it all; to know right and wrong, good and bad, beautiful and ugly. To feel profound emotions of love and hate, joy and discouragement, wonder, hope, and gratitude; to reason and plan my life in ways that accomplish things. Then best of all is to find all these wonderful human capacities caught up in knowing, loving, and serving the greatest being in the universe; our Maker, our Savior, and our God. It was one of those rare moments like a brief brush with eternity.

I guess the really big basic human questions that must have been asked in the early church: "Who are you," and, "What your ultimate purpose in life is?" Have you ever wondered who you are? No dog or rare turtle, fish or squirrel, beloved cat or bird; ever lost one peaceful night's sleep thinking about the fundamental questions. Only humans wistfully ask the specific questions. Only humans kill themselves and knowingly kill willing others when they don't get true and satisfying answers to the questions.

When we carefully consider this, we usually place the proper emphasis on ourselves, but what if we sympathetically view these questions from another angle or perspective? In divine essence, "See yourself the way God naturally sees you." Peter, as he explains to his converts how special they are to God. Everyone popularly knew the Israelites were precisely God's chosen people, but these Gentiles wanted to know who they were? And Peter said thoughtfully, conforming to verse 9 of First Peter, chapter 2.

He says,

"But ye are a chosen generation, a royal priesthood, a holy nation, a peculiar people; that ye should show forth the praises of him who hath called you out of darkness into his marvelous light."

This familiar verse adequately provides a direct contrast to the previous verse, a terrific contrast between those who sincerely believe in Jesus Christ and those who do not. We rightfully belong to God (For example, God chose us, but we did not choose God. And because he has chosen us, we can gratefully accept what God has faithfully done for us):

1. **We Are A Chosen Generation;** Chosen means selected by God for a special purpose, Jesus was voluntarily chosen by God to be the Cornerstone of the Christian. It was by divine plane. Sufficient evidence of First Peter 2:6 which says politely, **"Behold, I lay in Zion a chief corner stone, elect, precious: and he that believeth on him shall not be disappointed."**

2. **We Are Chosen To Be A Royal Priesthood;** faithful believers are transformed not only internally, but also externally. In First Peter 2:5 it says humbly, **"And now you are living stones that are being used to build a spiritual house. You are also a group of holy priests, and with the help of Jesus Christ you will offer sacrifices that please God."** In divine essence, we naturally become a spiritual house, and what does this sincerely mean? That our luminous bodies respectively become the dedicated temple of the living God; because, First Corinthians 3:16 says earnestly, **"Know ye not that ye are the temple of God, and that the Spirit of God dwelleth in you?"** In the Old Testament, God dwelt fondly in the tabernacle; and in the New Testament, God dwells fondly in our human body. He instantly becomes us and we become Him. We are a local priesthood that continuous functions in a ruling capacity, as mighty kings; because we are dearly bought with a price (see First Corinthians 6:20).

3. **We Are Chosen To Be A Holy Nation;** as Son's and Daughter's of God, (In essence, born again believers.) we are a unified group of people who are set apart for God's use.

4. **We Are Chosen To Be A Peculiar People;** God protects those whom He has adopted into His family. The word "a" in our text verse serves as a modifier of a noun; it is used to identify special individuals, those who have a relationship with Jesus Christ. Those who are chosen by God dragged out of the gutter of humanity; given a purpose to intercede on behalf of God's children. And called to reach those in darkness and bring them to the light.

However, without God people would not have any spiritual illumination. It is important to note:

That which is perishable takes on imperishable.
That which is in dishonor takes on everlasting honor.
That which is weak gently takes on divine power.
That which is natural takes on spiritual.
That which is mortal willingly takes on immortality.
That which is dead takes on life.

And that which is characterized by faith has done well in obedience to God. Real "faith" is a lifestyle that is consistently pleasing, not simply something you do for two hours on Sundays! This kind of "faith" is so rare God is conducting a global search: What kind of a "faith-person" are you? Whichever one you are the Scripture tells you to, "Examine yourself!" Test yourself daily to see if your faith is genuine and trust the Holy Spirit to do three (3) things:

- **Illuminate your mind:** Remember all lost souls are in spiritual darkness (see 2 Corinthians 4:3, 4).
- **Prick your heart:** As Peter preached Christ the willing listeners, **"They were pricked in their dear hearts"** (Acts 2:37). The word 'pricked' mean to pierce or cut to open, penetrate or soak in.
- **Voluntarily change your conscious will:** The prodigal son returned home when he came to himself and said thoughtfully, **"I will arise and go to my Father"** (Luke 15:18). The kind word 'arise' instantly tells us that the homeward journey to God is always upward, while that with Satan is always downward.

More to the key point, Peter began carefully to gently wrap this up; he respectfully informs us to accurately report our abundant evidence:

5. **We Are Chosen To Be A Witness;** consequently, that means precisely telling our beloved story. We may not be up-to-date in all modern techniques of gentle soul winning. And maybe able to quote correctly the necessary

scriptures without a flaw, but if we just tell our remarkable story. What is our story? We must tell all the wonderful things that God has willingly done. The peaceful purpose for our having been miraculously transformed into these marvelous wonders is our glorious God. We must tell them that Christ's cross is where earthly glory died and the world is stripped of its charms and the problem of human redemption is solved. We must tell them that the cross has multiplied the twelve who love each other into countless millions who dearly love one another. We must tell them and show them the love of God so full that they will come willing to take up the cross and follow Jesus daily. We must tell them that the wicked and righteous are different in distinctive character and mind. In (Isaiah 5:20) God said fiercely, **"Woe unto them that call evil good, and good evil; that put darkness for light and light for darkness; that put bitter for sweet and sweet for bitter."** Does it sound familiar? So we must tell them that Jesus came to this world of sin and shame, hung, bled and died. But early the third day morning, He rose obediently with glorious victory and divine power.

And then all at once, I fondly recall my dear mother's encouraging words. And they have always carefully followed me. They have clung persistently to me.

"Oh! Ray my dear boy," said she, "If you do this, you will be wise and successful in everything you do."

Notice below if you will:

The Three Things My Dear Mother Told Me

"This book of the law shall not depart out of thy mouth; but thou shalt meditate therein day and night, that thou mayest observe to do according to all that is written therein: for then thou shalt make thy way prosperous, and then thou shalt have good success" (Joshua 1:8).

In a favorable view of this sentimental verse, my late Mom and Dad, typically hold a special place in my dear heart. Because of the unique way, they have naturally influenced my life. Many of us are successful today, not because we are so wonderful, so smart, so beautiful, or so courageous. We are successful because of our parents, grandparents and others, both men and women, who took the place of absent parents. Many of them fasted, prayed, and interceded on our behalf. God has blessed us to be successful in order to reach back and empower the next generation. If we refuse to teach, train, prepare and empower our young men and women, we will be responsible for contributing to the moral, spiritual and intellectual destruction of a major part of God's gender. To those who wish to be technical about it. There are naturally many remarkable things my dear parents, grandparents, and spiritual parents politely told me; far too numerous to mention here.

But however, graciously allow me to elaborate on three of the most authentic things my dear mother said to me.

1. The loving words my dear mother said to me: **Tell me who you been with, and I'll tell you what you been doing.**

    •   Bad Company (you need to know who you're hanging out with)

    If we are going to be successful Christians we have to choose our friends wisely and carefully. According to First Corinthians 15:33 which says, **"Be not deceived: evil communications corrupt good manners."** What this means is that evil company corrupts good habits. You can read Judges Chapter (16); which presents the conclusion of the Samson stories. Samson's involvement with two more Philistine women is detailed here. According to verses (1, 2 and 3), it tells us how he flirted with a prostitute in Gaza, followed by another display of strength. Verses (4-22) deal with his foolish affair with Delilah, which led to his downfall. Yet the story ends with Samson's destruction of the Philistines' in their pagan temple. If we are going to be Christ-like children, we need to watch the company we keep.

For example: Many are incarcerated, thrown in jail, because of bad company. Some are kick out of school; have been rejected for promotions and possibly fired off their jobs, because of bad company.

Many are hospitalized, institutionalized, and are crippled for life; relationships are broken up; some are dead-fast asleep, because of bad company, and disgracefully the list goes on and on.

2. The loving words my dear mother said to me: **I'm not fattening frogs for snakes.**

- Positive Purpose (you need to understand your goal or your purpose for living)

If we are going to be successful Christians we have to keep our purpose in view (see Mark 7:24—30). Do you remember when Jesus was in the midst of teaching or feeding his disciples, in which he called his children? When the woman approached him, right in the middle of him feeding his children, but Jesus said unto her "let the children first be filled: for it is not proper to take the children's bread, and to cast it unto the dogs." In other words, Jesus was saying, during a meal one does not stop to feed the little dogs. Jesus is not attempting to insult the woman by using this illustration. In fact, he is testing her faith. Matthew record Jesus' reaction to her reply, "**O woman, great is your faith**" (Matthew 15:28). The woman understood Jesus' test and persistently replied that even during the meal the little dogs consumed the children's crumbs that fall from the table. Rewarding her persistence, Jesus granted her request. He cast the demons out of her daughter, although the little girl was not in his presence. Don't be afraid to believe that you can have what you want and deserve:

- Watch your thoughts they become your words.
- Watch your words, they become your actions.
- Watch your actions, they become your character.
- Watch your character, for it becomes your destiny.

Consequently, "**Death and life are in the power of the tongue: and they that love it shall eat the fruit thereof**" (Proverbs 18:21). As a direct result, those who constantly talk doubt; in profound effect, talk death. Faithful Christians who humbly speak the inspired Word of God speak everlasting life.

3. The loving words my dear mother said to me: **I have humbly prayed for you and now I have given you back to God.**

- Personal Relationship with God (you got to know the Lord for yourself)

If we are willingly going to be successful Christians, we must know Jesus Christ for ourselves. Daniel had previously been appointed a chosen governor in Babylon by Nebuchadnezzar. Here we instantly find that he insisted on praying to God rather than carefully avoiding the magnificent lion's private den. Daniel was frequently pushed to compromise his unbounded faith, but he didn't do it. Yet, Daniel naturally has had a personal relationship with God. Because Daniel sufficiently showed his abiding faith, King Nebuchadnezzar properly honored God. All the same, "How might your direct actions positively influence someone powerful to properly honor God?" We can properly develop our direct relationship with Jesus through humble prayer, Bible reading, and through Christian service. The possible way we get to know Jesus as our personal Savior is by carefully developing a public and private devotional life. Nevertheless, God has willingly promised that if we faithfully obey our dear parents, our moral lives will be graciously extended. If we faithfully obey, the spiritual parent God proper places over us; we will live longer, healthier, purposeful and more spiritually fulfilled lives. God has willingly promised he will bless and properly take care of us. Graciously allow me to willingly say in direct response to this teaching that I am determined to voluntarily join the poet-writer Civilla D. Martin. Who says enthusiastically, "God Will Take Care of You:

"Be not dismayed, whatever betides,
God will take care of you;
Beneath his wings of love abide,
God will take care of you;
No matter what may be the test?
God will take care of you;
Lean, weary one, upon God's breast,
God will take care of you;
God will take care of you,
Through every day, ore all the way;
God will take care of you; God will take care of you."

CHAPTER 2

NEVERTHELESS, CHRIST IS IN ME:

SOCIAL FELLOWSHIP

"I am crucified with Christ; nevertheless I live; yet not I, but Christ liveth in me; and the life which I now live in the flesh I live by the faith of the Son of God, who loved me, and gave himself for me" (Galatians 2:20; KJV).

2. THE BELIEVER'S POSITION — YOU MUST BE IN CHRIST:

To have a healthy, fulfilled, and happy relationship with the Son of God; always take the unique opportunity to:

a) Know Your Running Mate (you living in Christ, and Christ living in you)
b) Be Like-Minded (sharing the same or similar views, opinions, tastes, values, or outlook)
c) God himself shall be with you (come out from among them (unbelievers), and be ye separate (means separation but not isolation) —2 Corinthians 6:16.)

Questions for a Remarkable Transformation:

- Ask yourself who am I in Christ.
- How do I know that Christ is in me? (see Galatians 2:20, as I explain below)
- But what does it mean to have Christ living inside you? (In you—the dwelling place of God is with you—see 2 Corinthians 6:16; Revelation 21:3.)

To fellowship with God victoriously, you have to gratefully acknowledge your running mate. Once you have carefully planned out a fix—you need to do for yourself, I humbly suggest when you gently place your abiding faith in Christ; allow him to be the Lord of your life. Interestingly this accurately describes God in you.

Funny that I gratefully remember the joyous excitement of the first precious time I instantly discovered Christ was naturally in me. The absolute fulfillment of knowing there was no considerable distance between us. That glorious day, Jesus became more to me than a philosophical concept and more than a religious being that I intentionally tried to get closer to, He instantly became to me the very divine essence of who I am. The glorified Christ who unanimously adopted me as His dwelling place (It means to have Christ living inside you and gives you insight for living life with Christ.) He whispered gently to me,

"It is no longer you who live, but it is I, Christ, living in you; and the life that you now live in the flesh, you live by my faith."

I fondly remember running joyfully to a dresser mirror and gently leaning closer, looking deeply into my own eyes and dear heart, saying thoughtfully:

"I can see you, Jesus, you are right here, in me."

That awareness of Christ's indwelling generated an untiring energy within me to write and share Him with others also. I began witnessing Christ with whomever and whatever stood still long enough to hear me. It is the fellowship that I enjoy with the Father that compels me to communicate.

Please take a precious moment and ask yourself these direct questions:

- How does "guilt pang" naturally affect you?
- Is the terrible pain you have caused other people naturally becoming the personal hate you feel for yourself?

A Pang of Guilt

Most sensible people naturally gravitate towards one moral end of the visible spectrum of conscious guilt. On one willingly hand, some instantly see themselves as blameless and always right. Others have a tendency to beat themselves up over every little thing. If we look earnestly to God, we see that neither attitude is where he genuinely wants us to be. Instead, God wants us to gratefully acknowledge our mortal sins and sincerely repent. He wants us to gratefully accept his divine forgiveness, turn from our meaningful ways, but then we must move forward into God's mighty will for our dear lives.

However, I have learned there are certain keys to enjoying the will (blessings) of God on a daily basis. I sincerely thank God every glorious day that I am able to live peacefully in this notorious world. We must properly value the precious freedoms that we typically have and must be accurately determined that the clever devil will never steal them from me, you and our lovely families.

"There is therefore now no condemnation ("guilt") to them which are in Christ Jesus, who walk not after the flesh, but after the Spirit" (Romans 8:1).

There are certain Biblical keys that my wife, son, and I live by so that we may enjoy God's will in our lives. I want to share with you three vital keys that will bring a greater anointing of Jesus Christ into your life. Jesus taught that the first priority of every believer is to seek after the kingdom of God.

In the Holy Bible, (Matthew 6:33) Jesus says to you—me,

"But seek ye first the kingdom of God and his righteousness, and all these things shall be added unto you."

Nevertheless, the King James Bible tells us that it is not really the everyday things such as food, drink, and worldly possessions, (Romans 14:17) read,

"For the kingdom of God is not meat and drink, but righteousness, and peace, and joy in the Holy Ghost."

There are three keys that you should think about as you create this picture of your life in fellowship with God. This will give you a structure and foundation to build your spiritual life.

The Three Vital Keys to a Successful Life with God:

1. JOY

"Don't let the enemy steal your joy. Learn how to praise God through every circumstance whether good or bad. We must learn how to be thankful, not because of what we have, but because of who Jesus is to us." Praise God!

The apostle Paul taught the early church that,

"For the kingdom of God is not in word, but in power"
(1 Corinthians 4:20).

2. THE POWER OF THE HOLY GHOST

The early believers were filled and anointed with the Spirit. The Holy Ghost produced the power that released miracles in their lives. Jesus said that the precious Holy Ghost would help you in three areas of your life: "Lead, Guide and Comfort."

And also in the Holy Bible, Jesus says:

"These things I have spoken unto you, that in me ye might have peace. In the world ye shall have tribulation: but be of good cheer; I have overcome the world" (John 16:33).

The Spirit of God is the Spirit of Truth. Earlier in this chapter, Jesus is referred to as the Comforter. He also shows us things to come. Therefore, we are never at the mercy of the attacks of the enemy.

3. WE HAVE THE NAME OF JESUS

We have the authority of Jesus himself backed by all of heaven great strength. His name is our credentials of authority. The devil has to obey the Word of God. He cannot cut you off from God's love and power. That is why we need to stay filled with the Spirit of God.

In the Message (MSG) Bible, it has this to say about, (Matthew 10:39),

"Of your first concern is to look after yourself, you'll never find yourself. But if you forget about yourself and look to me (your Lord, God), you'll find both yourself and me."

As a result of which, God says the only way you're ever going to find yourself is by forgetting yourself and focusing on Him. Then you'll not only figure out God; you'll also figure out you. That's what it means to live like Jesus or to demonstrate your identity as a person of Him.

Christ the Son is the same essence as God the Father and this was made visible to us, and given to us as well. Upon which our fellowship with Christ guarantees fellowship with the Father. In the New King James Version of the Holy Bible, it has this to say about (First John 1:3),

"That which we have seen and heard declare we unto you, that ye also may have fellowship with us: and truly our fellowship is with the Father, and with his Son Jesus Christ."

At heart, the primary reason John writes is to provide us with an understanding of what we must do to have fellowship with the apostles and God. Fellowship carries both the idea of a positive relationship that people share and participation in a common interest or goal. The fellowship John promotes is not only vertical, between the believer and God. He writes that they may have fellowship "with us." It was the reality of Christ in me that drove me to make others aware of the wealth that was within their reach also. Many experiences can lose their thrill after a while, but the awareness of God's indwelling only grows in its appeal and intensity. Speaking from the reality of an awareness of your union with Christ; the reality of a living relationship with Him, is irresistible and it is all the qualification you will ever need.

Many of the disciples Jesus chose were illiterate. And the few who learned to write, did not bother putting anything on record until decades after His death and resurrection. The simple reason for this is that Christ in them was a reality of much greater importance to them than systematic theology. Bible scripture (Acts, chapter 4 and verse 13) speaks,

> *"Now when they saw the boldness of Peter and John, and perceived that they were unlearned and ignorant men, they marveled; and they took knowledge of them, that they had been with Jesus."*

At this key point, even though Peter and John were uneducated Galilean fishermen, they spoke with endless confidence and genuine freedom. Their unique presentation of the glorious gospel was powerful because they were personal witnesses of everything they spoke about. It is imperative to understand your qualification to witness for Christ has nothing to do with your moral education or social status; it has everything in common to do with your direct contact with Jesus. Paul the one apostle that could boast of his gifted education and human qualifications had this to say earnestly about it:

> *"But what thing were gain to me, those I counted loss for Christ" (Philippians 3:7).*

You genuinely see those outstanding things that Paul believed to be important became unimportant after willingly encountering the resurrected Messiah. The same credentials these intelligent people are waving around as something elite. I'm tearing up and throwing out with the trash, along with everything else I properly used to take credit for. Why, Paul? Because of Christ:

"Yea doubtless, and I count all things but loss for the excellency of the knowledge of Christ Jesus my Lord: for whom I have suffered the loss of all things, and do count them but dung, that I may win Christ" (Philippians 3:8).

Oh, the moral value of knowing precisely Christ surpasses all else (see Philippians 2:3; 4:7). Everything I once thought I had in common been going carefully for me is insignificant. I've allegedly dumped it all in the trash so that I could embrace Christ.

In (First Peter 3:15) it says politely,

"But sanctify the Lord God in your hearts: and be ready always to give an answer to every man that asketh you a reason of the hope that is in you with meekness and fear."

Therefore, let me voluntarily share with you my personal testimony. I grew up in a small town in Arkansas, carefully reared in the private home of my deceased parents: Sarah and Jerry (JW). Dad and Mom struggled along like most others of that time and place, working hard, paying bills, trying to make ends meet. Thank God for two fanatical parents. At the age of eleven, I heard Pastor W. L. Debro deliver his sermon. I then felt that I was not saved; when the invitation was given for church members and sinners to come forward for prayer. I embraced the first opportunity, knowing that I needed a great work done to fit me for heaven. My soul was thirsting of full and free salvation but knew not how to obtain it. Shortly after being taught repentance of sin; I was converted and baptized. I voluntarily changed or rather the Holy Spirit willingly helped me to radically change. I cannot thoughtfully say what I was precisely at that moral point. Granting to evangelical thought, I was saved. I know now this was the beginning of the path to a brand-new life in Christ.

However, I fell by the wayside as a young adult, lost, confused, and disconnected. As I have indicated previously. Just when I genuinely thought I had everything under control, needless to say thoughtfully, I thought I naturally had it going on. I had the perfect job: sat comfortably behind my polished desk and properly made key decisions, responsible for knowingly hiring and firing, or come and go willingly as I wonderfully pleased. Yes, I undoubtedly had the neatest car around. I didn't have rims like some of my acquaintances. I just kept my lovely car clean both inside and out, and to me; it was undoubtedly the neatest on the logical block. Certainly, my apartment was fully furnished with the finest of furniture. And ooh, let me tell you, I was dressed from head to toe; but at the blink of an eye, I lost my job, my car, and out of nowhere came a big fire and took everything I ever owned. For me, life had caved in.

However, it is very important to popularly know lovely things can change overnight. And when remarkable things change for the worse, you've instantly got to be able to carefully shake it off. Precious time is instantly filled with swift transition, so build your moral hopes, not on precious money, for example:

- The money will dearly buy a luxurious bed, but it will not buy a peaceful sleep.
- The dear money will buy food, but not a hearty appetite.
- The money will dearly buy modern-day medicine, but not everyday health.
- The money will dearly buy a lovely house, but not a humble home.
- The dear money will eagerly buy a diamond ring, but it will not buy genuine love.
- The dear money will promptly buy a church pew, but it will not buy eternal salvation.

Therefore you'd better build your ultimate hopes on things eternal and hold to God's unchanging hand.

Presently (right now) if you died today, where would you spend eternity? Gratefully remember it is one or the other: merciful heaven or eternal hell? As a former law enforcement professional, I was regularly confronted by possible death, and the fundamental question constantly entered my conscious mind. Please, willingly take this key moment to naturally think about it; I intellectually challenge you to acknowledge thoughtfully the fundamental question: Where do you want to willingly spend eternity? It is either merciful heaven or eternal hell? I was once told heaven and hell does not exist; yet, the well-worn Bible has much to say thoughtfully on the fundamental question.

"Is heaven and hell real?"

Some likely people may act in response by answering "no!"

"There is no sufficient proof; no one has been to heaven or hell and came back to instantly tell about it."

"Have you ever been to heaven?"

"Or, have you ever been to hell?" A dear lady once asked me.

Without a reasonable doubt, the infallible Holy Bible properly instructs the devout believer that heaven and hell is real. Eternal heaven is the spiritual dwelling house place of God. It is where all true and remnant Christians will go after death provided we stay faithful throughout this moral life: (Read Revelation 21, this devoted chapter refer to: "The New Heaven; the New Earth and the New Jerusalem.")

We will have new bodies and new experiences according to (1Corinthians 15:35-57); the faithful believer's works will be judged at the "chief Judgment seat of Christ" (see 2 Corinthians 5:1-10); and this judgment will take place in the air, following the first resurrection. The honored dead in eternal Christ shall rise first according to (1 Thessalonians 4:14-18).

What do you naturally think of when you instantly hear the word hell? Here, underneath are eight reasonable meditate philosophical thought:

- A place deep down under the raw surface of the hardened earth

- A bottomless pit

- A burning lake of terrible fire

- A terrible place where the Devil and wicked demons dwell unduly

- A dreadful place of brutal torture for the wicked souls of exposed humans

- A terrible place of the wicked dead

- An immoral region

- A dreadful place properly called the criminal underworld.

However, eternal hell is a terrible place of eternal separation from God, merely prepared for the wicked devil and his avenging angels. It is a dreadful place of eternal torment, (see precisely Matthew 25:46). Specific words uniquely related to everlasting hell naturally include Gehenna, Hades, Sheol, and a shallow grave.

Nevertheless, the word hell appears prominently in the King James Bible 54 considerable times, 31 times in the Old Testament and 23 times in the New Testament. At some point after the final judgment, all who have not been granted the personal gift of eternal life will be cast into the "Lake of Fire;" which is the second terrible death. And which results in their total destruction. You typically see the possible way to miraculously escape this second death is to be properly found, on the very final Day of Judgment; to be "in Christ Jesus," granting to (Revelation 20:6).

Nevertheless, as you humbly acknowledge the genuine greatness of God; our Father and our Savior, the Lord Jesus Christ as your personal Redeemer; it is essential for you to carefully keep in mine. We have been voluntarily taking on His remarkable peculiarities such as His' unique identity. Indeed, (Titus 2:14) speak of Him.

It has this to say,

"Who gave himself for us, that He might redeem us from all iniquity, and purify unto Himself a peculiar people, zealous of good works."

Typically signifying that what He did on the Cross; Christ in mutual agreement for every personal sin past, present, and glorious future; at least for all who will sincerely believe (John 3:16),

"For God so loved the world that he gave his only begotten Son, that whosoever believeth in him should not perish, but have everlasting life."

The sanctified life is strictly within the proper boundaries of the ultimate sacrifice of Christ, which must eternally stay the direct object of our enduring faith.

Yet, as I prominently mentioned memorable moments ago, I shared in common with you the direct questions that were humbly asked of me: "Have you eternally been to angelic heaven?" Or, "Have you ever been to everlasting hell?" In illustrated fact, these are wonderfully intriguing questions; nevertheless, definitely through my dear Lord and Savior Jesus Christ during the year 1985. I mean instantly, my precious soul was taken out of my graceful body. I went instantly with Jesus up out of my gorgeous bed and into the unclouded sky. It was as though I had died peacefully, and my lovely body was left behind on the bed. While my kindred spirit was going carefully with Jesus, up through to the visible top of the dear house. It seemed as though the whole roof was pulled back, and I kept going higher and higher into angelic heaven; yet, through the divine Power of His Holy Spirit. From practical side to side, the ultimate end to end and all the way through, God progressively changes me for the better. By miraculously transforming me into the express image of His Son Jesus Christ. He genuinely wants to sufficiently develop me into a better and more holy person; both on the inside and the outside (see Romans 12:2). The well-worn Holy Bible tells me that one of the highest, goals that God has in store for me is my unique transformation in Him. This remarkable transformation is realistically accomplished by the renewing of my conscious mind.

Now, Philippians 2:5 wraps up this striking illustration by saying thoughtfully,

"Let this mind be in you, which was also in Christ Jesus."

(This verse refers to the peculiarities of Christ, and portrays Him as the supreme example).

In the Book of Jonah, we read carefully of him God's inspired prophet who was typically cast into the deep sea. I talked about in my recent book out of the prominent belly of a burning hell, "Alive, I Cried Fiercely." He was swallowed up by a gigantic fish. And Jonah was precisely in the prominent belly of the great monster (private hell) three miserable days and three sultry nights.

Graciously allow me to earnestly discuss with you a personal experience from my own life about my intense trip:

To Hell and Back

All the same, life is as overwhelming as my emotionally overpowering visit to hell. During the course of being robbed at gunpoint in the year 2011; Jesus spoke with me and said I am going to take you by my Spirit into private hell. Then, all of a sudden, the gunman begins shouting in fierce strife with an intimidating voice:

"Carefully give me all your money, or I will kill you!"

"This day you're going to die!" he said vehemently.

In unbounded amazement, I looked thoughtfully at this evil heart and naturally wondered what its personal purpose was merely. Jesus said, essentially, as he ushering me down into the private realm of the mighty dead. There was nothing but deep moonless darkness all around me; it was unpleasant, and an unlikable site to see of the complete emptiness of yelling furiously and burnings. In the midst of me merely preaching the affirmed gunman came running to gratefully receive the precious gift of Salvation by sincere repentance.

Then I graciously heard the pleasant voice of the dear Lord as he was politely asking, "Will you willingly receive this dear man an evildoer?"

And I said eagerly, "Yes!" merely raising my authoritative voice slightly to be scarcely heard over the hideous noises and looking around, "Is a miserable place!"

Instantly, I was brought back by his Spirit into that shocking communal experience of glorious victory. As a precise result, this is undoubtedly an outer body encounter. And the divine Word of God properly teaches the body without the spirit is dead; although Jesus was precisely with me.

Yet, the undeniable fact of the matter is the devil walks about like a roaring lion, typically attempting whom he may eagerly devour (see 1 Peter 5:8). Just as he naturally did in Job's historic day going to and fro upon the dear earth.

Jesus said in the Bible scripture (John 15:4), and he steadfastly insists you abide in him.

Indeed, the dear Lord's divine Word says thoughtfully,

"Abide in me, and O in you. As the branch cannot bear fruit of itself, except it abide in the Vine; no more can ye- (you), except ye- (you) abide in me."

Please, take note of abiding in him correctly refer to the remarkable fact that we gratefully recognize every possible solution we desperately try to find; for whatever the specific need might be, is found only just in Jesus Christ. We must never be separated from him.

In Ephesians 4:9, the dear apostle Paul unanimously confirms,

"Now that He ascended, what is it but that He also descended first into the lower parts of the earth."

It is important for you to see likely first he went down into Paradise meaning (The realm of the believing dead, known as the grave of the saints; this was believed to be the Old Paradise of God during the Old Testament time.) to deliver all the believing souls in that region. During that modern time Paradise (the Old Testament Saints) was situated close to the realm of the unbelieving dead; reserved for judgment (see 2 Peter 2:4).

This specific area was once in the direct vicinity of the Old Paradise of God; now Satan uses it (by express permission only) entirely for his evil purposes. Where one precious day he will be tormented like anyone else, those who reject Jesus Christ as Lord and Savior (see Matthew 5:22, 29-30; 10:28; 16:18). This holding area was necessary since the Old Testament sacrifices did not take away mortal sins but only covered them. Throughout the Old Testament, there is the moral teaching of a holding area for the faithful as well as for the unfaithful. Abraham in (Genesis 25:8) says when he died he gathered to his dear people. David said that when his beloved son died (2 Samuel 12:28) I will go to him, he will not come to me. Jacob said in (Genesis 49:29) I was to be gathered to my people. A definite location was being spoken passionately of.

The New Testament term "After Christ's glorious resurrection," indicates precisely Paradise was moved to eternal heaven. Graciously according to its original state because Paradise was properly divided by a mighty chasm, gulf (see Luke 16). God willingly allows this Angel to give the private key of the unlimited pit (The private realm of the unbelieving dead; the marked grave and everlasting hell) to Satan in (Revelation 20:1-2); where he was shut up, properly sealed, and intimately bound for a thousand years. Now, he is loosened out and about. Roaming the illuminated face of the created earth, looking eagerly for someone (like you and me) to eat up.

Eternal paradise and dear heaven are the same places, and we find the specific location is "up" (see 2 Kings 2:1—11; 2 Corinthians 12:2). As well as an eternal place of magnificent residence for those who trust in God (see Luke23:43). Willingly allow it forever be understood that God made eternal heaven and perpetual hell.

In the well-worn Bible, Ephesians 3:9-13 states,

"And to make all men see what is the fellowship of the mystery, which from the beginning of the world hath been hid in God, who created all things by Jesus Christ: To the intent that now unto the principalities and powers in heavenly places might be known by the church the manifold wisdom of God, according to the eternal purpose which he purposed in Christ Jesus our Lord: in whom we have boldness and access with confidence by the faith of him. Wherefore I desire that ye faint not at my tribulation for you, which is your glory."

You naturally see, to bring to light something which had previously been hidden; could be faithfully translated, "The doctoral fellowship of the merciful dispensation of the Revelation of the Mystery." In other kind words, the Mystery is no more, having instantly been revealed by and through Jesus Christ our dear Lord and what he did at the Cross. Because of his Atoning Work on the Cross, we can presently enjoy extraordinary boldness in our profound "faith."

Therefore let us get up and go carefully, above and beyond ourselves; day or night, to the direct call of moral duty; faithfully serving the hungry and thirsty hearts among us. As we gratefully recognize his divine call to gently follow. And when our glorious time has been amply fulfilled, may we naturally gather into the pearly gates of eternal paradise to be with our dear Lord forever?

Being Redeemed

Indeed,

"Christ hath redeemed us from the curse of the law,
(redeemed meaning brought back) being made a curse for us:
for it is written, Cursed is every one that hangeth on a tree"
(Galatians 3:13):

(Now colon (:) punctuation, properly meaning we naturally need to talk earnestly about this.) So in proper order for us to understand correctly, willingly allow me to humbly propose this hypothetical question: Have you absolutely thought about what it sincerely means to be redeemed? You typically see, to genuinely follow eternal redemption (which possibly means the moral state of being redeemed); you must properly recognize that before you are miraculously saved; you are a slave to sin. And being a slave to sin, you have no choice. You are on your way to everlasting hell and sin has you hanging by the meaty neck. This is why we carefully develop such moral problems in our local churches; in our independent schools; in our lovely homes, and on our suitable jobs. This is why we do the low–down things we do to one another. This is why there is such a drug problem. Those who are knowingly hired to voluntarily stop it become typically involved in it. This is why we have such a drinking problem in the world today; because the responsible person outside of Christ is a slave to sin.

In the well-worn Holy Bible, Romans 6:16 says thoughtfully,

"Know ye not, that to whom ye yield yourselves servants to obey, his servants ye are to whom ye obey?"

What this means is that Paul highlights the fundamental principle that everyone is a slave to someone or something; whether it is a responsible person, prized possession or economic activity. You are undoubtedly either a faithful servant of God or a servant of Satan. There is no in between. It is one or the countless other. The modern world is hungry for the Living Bread. We genuinely need to lift the Savior up for them to correctly see. We dearly need to humbly trust him and do not doubt the passionate -words that he said thoughtfully.

"If I am lifted up, I will naturally draw, all men unto me."
I don't mean to sound so inquisitive, but it's essential we properly understand that Jesus is our redeemer.
We have a choice. We can typically attempt to live peacefully this dear life by either law or faith. We cannot live peacefully by both.

Paul clearly states in Galatians, chapter 3 and verse 13, the descriptive paragraph (a) of this independent clause. He says,

"Christ hath redeemed us from the curse of the law."

What this means my Christians friends is that Jesus' death paid for our sins and delivers us from the bondage of sin upon our acceptance of Him. The infallible Bible abundantly illustrates that Galatians 3:13, those who attempt to be morally justified through 'the creative works of the moral law,' are cursed. Paul and every believer were crucified with Christ in order to die to sin (the law). Although we live on physically, almighty Christ also active lives within us spiritually. Because when a person naturally becomes a Christian, the Spirit of God rushes in and instantly makes the spiritual nature function. Christ's resurrection power through the Spirit is worked out through the Christian, who willingly chooses to live peacefully by lasting faith in the Son of God.

Paul states in Galatians 3:13, the key paragraph "b" of this proper clause,

"Being made a curse for us."

What this means is precisely that Jesus respectively became a fulfilled curse in our proper place. Granting to Bible scripture Second Corinthians 5:21 declare,

"For he (God) hath made him (Jesus) to be sin for us, who knew no sin, that we (you and me) might be made the righteousness of God in him."

Man, not willing to accept God's remedy for his destruction, tries to bring about his own salvation by human means:

- He tries for self-righteousness when he needs to be made the faithfulness of God.
- He tries to reform, when he needs to be regenerated.
- He tries to turn over a new leaf, when he needs a new life.
- He tries to be justified by the law, when he needs to be justified by faith in the Lord Jesus Christ.
- He tries to clean up the old man, when he needs to be made a new man in Christ.
- He tries to be saved by good works when he needs salvation by the grace of God.

The only remedy for the destruction of man is the Son of God, being made sin for us on the cross. And the only way to receive this remedy is by faith in Him as our personal Saviour. Then stepping out in it; stepping out in faith means that we pray, and trust, knowing that everything depends upon God. Then live as if we are doing everything we should be doing for Him. And if we do we will find that the Lord will always provide a way for us, as long as we are willing to step out in faith and move forward for His Glory. In order for us to take this step of faith, we have to confront our fears. Fears keep us from moving forward. So what is our key problem? Our dreadful fear will instantly tell us. Just ask yourself this basis question: What is it that naturally produces genuine fear in me? Especially when I think of voluntarily leaving it behind and stepping out in abiding faith? We need to back up and reassess what we are doing for the Lord. As we back up let us, carefully prepare to go forward in the dear Lord, by embracing God's guiding principles:

- Reaching Up, To Worship God
- Reaching Out, Dedicated To Serve Others
- Reaching In, Dedicated To Grow Together

Paul says thoughtfully in a welcome addition to Galatians 3:13 the descriptive paragraphs "c" and "d" of this independent clause. He says earnestly,

"For it is written, cursed is every one that hangeth on a tree."

For example, according to the Law of Moses, in the Book of Deuteronomy 21:23, this Message speaks,

"Anyone who is nailed to a tree is under a curse."

And being nailed to a tree was an Old Testament symbol of humiliation. He was treated as guilty, accused and cursed in our place. The curse came upon Him as our Substitute.

Paul says in Colossians 1:14,

"On whom we have redemption through His blood, the forgiveness of sins."

Let us look thoughtfully at the word "redemption." What does redemption mean? To carefully make a long story short, redemption means redeeming (saving us from sin). Therefore, through the cross (the glorious gospel, the good news of Jesus Christ, His innocent death), we have eternal redemption. Through the empty tomb (His glorious resurrection), we have eternal redemption:

- God has redeemed us from the terrible curse.
- God has redeemed us from the slavery of sin.
- God has given us the well-worn Bible in order that we might deny ourselves, take up our cross and follow Him.

He summoned the crowd with His disciples and said to them. 'If anyone wishes to come after me, he must deny himself, and take up his cross and follow me.' We can take up our cross; we can give up the world and walk with Jesus; or we can take up our faith, and fall into the temptation of the world and lose our soul. What I am earnestly trying to properly convey to you is that; we must accomplish the work of him that sent us while it is the day, for night cometh when no man can work. My dear brother or precious sister willingly let nothing separate you from the pleasing life and the eternal salvation of Jesus Christ. Jesus insists earnestly that cross-bearing is as essential, a key part of discipleship as faithful obedience or humble prayer or worship.

One Holy Spirit, But Many Operations

The Seven Divine Spirits of God

"And the spirit of the Lord shall rest upon him, the spirit of wisdom and understanding, the spirit of counsel and might, the spirit of knowledge and of the fear of the Lord."
(Isaiah 11:2).

The Holy Spirit (typically meaning the Spirit of Truth) faithfully gives spiritual gifts and god-fearing characteristics called the sevenfold aspect of the successful operations of the divine character of God outlined here in verse 2 (see Isaiah chapter 11). This shows the saintly perfections of the Holy Spirit in all his attributes listed here resting upon Jesus Christ (The Messiah; the soon coming Savior).

Consequently, this intelligent expression "The Seven Divine Spirits of God" does not refer to seven different spirits. It respectively refers to the various ways the Spirit of God expresses himself.

This devoted section is a study in direct contrast to the Seven Divine Spirits of God, who have been sent instantly (working faithfully) into all the dear world, we carefully defined: The notable first is who he is, "The Spirit of the dear Lord (That is, the spirit of **"mercy, and grace, and long-suffering, and abundance of goodness and truth, and forgiving iniquity and transgression and sin; for that is the Lord,** Exodus 34:6-7." While key aspects 2–7 are precisely what He is naturally? Here in (Isaiah 11:2); however, we gratefully recognize the way the Spirit of God works with a responsible person. These spiritual matters are clearly mentioned in the well-worn Old Testament Bible (Isaiah 11:3–5). The Seven Spirits of God naturally refer to the Holy Spirit. Therefore, he instantly reveals the fullness, the completeness of the divine Spirit of God. In other sacred words, he accurately represents the full and complete proof of the Holy Spirit in all his unique characteristics; in all completed phases of the remarkable diversities of his direct operations. They are also mentioned in the infallible New Testament Bible, the Book of Revelation four precious times:

- Revelation 1:4; mentions that the seven divine spirits are before God's mighty throne.
- Revelation 3:1; indicates Jesus Christ hold the seven spirits of God.
- Revelation 4:5; typically links the seven divine spirits of God with seven burning lamps that are before God's eternal throne.
- Revelation 5:6; positively identifies the seven divine spirits with the 'seven eyes' of the Lamb and states that they are sent out into the dear earth.

Below, briefly, in Isaiah Chapter 11; I will willingly share with you the three compromised keys needed in drawing close to God:

a) <u>The Life of the Christian</u>: Isaiah 11:1, **"And there shall come forth a rod out of the stem of Jesse** (the stem meaning derive, ancestry, or descendant)**, and a Branch** (meaning the Christian) **shall grow out of his roots."** Now, what this select verse means is that Jesus a descendant of David's princely family will someday be King and bear fruit. This excellent verse speaks enthusiastically about the fulfilled Messianic promise of the coming Messiah, the Savior. The well-worn Bible scripture Acts 13:23 read, **"Of this man's seed hath God according to his promise raised unto Israel** (referring to his children; the children of God) **a Savior, Jesus."** At this moment, let's properly refer to Matthew 1:21, **"And she shall bring forth a son, and thou shalt call his name Jesus** (meaning precisely the Savior)**: for he shall save his people from their sins."** What this means in more specific detail is that the Christian is not the humble root. We are not the mighty trunk. We are simply the local branches that are from this sacred tree. In John 15:5, Jesus says impressively, **"I am the vine, ye** (meaning morally you and me) **are the branches: He that abideth in me, and I in him, the same bringeth forth much fruit: for without me ye can do nothing."** Divine power and glorious vision for the local church undoubtedly derives from Christ, not the modern church. God's willingly people naturally depend upon Christ.

b) <u>The Spirit in the Christian</u>: Isaiah 11:2, **"And the spirit of the Lord shall rest upon him, the spirit of wisdom and understanding, the spirit of counsel and might, the spirit of knowledge and of the fear of the Lord."** Now, in this descriptive verse we discover the proper key to instantly comprehending the eternal life of Christ. When we look earnestly at his life as revealed in the canonical Gospels; I instantly recognize that God used him in an amazing way ministering to the dear people. Just think how you and I could step carefully into the same situations as Christ made, but voluntarily leave any real long-lasting worthy impact. We naturally need to be on top of that like almighty Christ our dear Lord.

c) <u>The Walk of the Christian</u>: Isaiah 11:3-5 says carefully," **And shall make him of quick** (immediately) **understanding in** the fear of the Lord: and he shall not judge after the sight of his eyes, neither reprove after the hearing of his ears: But with righteousness shall he judge the poor, and reprove with equity for the meek of the earth: and he shall smite the earth with the red rod of his mouth, and with the breath of his lips shall he slay the wicked." (Intentionally meaning the worthy poor and the needy will be properly treated with divine fairness and justice. His sacred word will continue being precisely the official law everywhere in the fertile land, and wicked doers will be put to death). "And righteousness shall be the girdle of his loins and faithfulness the girdle of his reins." Righteousness, honesty, and fairness will be confined to him; under his control (see Ephesians 6:14; Isaiah 25:1). When a humble person is Spirit–dependent, he will live life differently. Although we might properly treat these graceful verses as only applying to the eternal life of the Savior Jesus Christ; we are reasonably expected to make the logical conclusion that if we willingly share in the anointing, then we share in the creative works that stem from that anointing. We are to live as Christ's faithful disciples. The highly regarded disciple of Christ not only has divine Master's superior knowledge but also mighty power.

Abiding In Love

"As the Father hath loved me, so have I loved you; continue ye in my love," (Saint John 15:9; KJV).

It is altogether agreed that Christ's meaningful conversation in this humorous verse and the following chapter was at the delightful close of his Last Supper; the memorable night in which he was betrayed. Now that he was about to voluntarily leave the beloved disciples, they would be tempted to grow strange to one another. And therefore carefully he presses it upon them to genuinely love one another.

So many precious times we willingly allow that little word hate to come in and traditionally separate us. If we are to be successful Christians, we must faithfully follow the humble God way of brotherly love. God is love granting to First John 4:8. If we keep on loving one another we will stay one in our hearts with God, and he will stay one with us. If we truly love one another and live as Jesus did in this creative world. We won't be worried about the Day of Judgment, as mentioned in chapter 3. So therefore, "Repent of Any Sin." A genuine love for others will chase those economic worries away.

When we think carefully of Christ's meaningful conversation with his beloved disciples, let us instantly notice three vital characteristics:

1. The Father's Love for his Son:

"As the Father hath loved me," he genuinely loved him as Mediator; this is my beloved Son, in whom I am well pleased. He was the Son of his unconditional love. He dearly loved him and willingly gave all remarkable things unto his dear hands. He continually loved his Father and was beloved of him. Even when he was made sin and curse for us and it wonderfully pleased the dear Lord to bruise him, yet, he abode in the Father's unconditional love. He went cheerfully through his unspeakable sufferings, and therefore his Father continued to love him. Notice, it was essential for Christ to abide in his Father's love.

a) <u>Obedience was required</u>: He abode in his Father's Love because he kept His Father's divine law; according to verse 10 of the context (see John chapter 15), which says, **"I have kept my Father's commandments, and abide in his love."** To genuinely love God, we first must be obedient to his divine Word. God's children love God's well-worn Bible. God's Bible is a remarkable letter carefully written to his beloved children and the more often we read diligently it, the more often we graciously hear from him.

The Bible is also a mighty weapon. It is called, "the precious sword of the Spirit." You genuinely need this loaded weapon in your continual warfare against Satan. When Jesus was tempted, he picked up the sword and drove the devil back. The psalmist said thoughtfully, **"Thy word have I hid in mine heart, that I might not sin against thee, Psalm 119:11."**

Hereby he showed he continued to love his Father that, he went on and went through with his undertaking. Therefore, the Father continued to love him. In Isaiah 42 it says enthusiastically, "His dear soul delighted in him because he did not fail, and nor was he discouraged."

2. The Son's Love for his Disciples:

a) <u>The consistent pattern of his unconditional love</u>: **"As the Father hath loved me, so have I loved you."** An unusual expression of the condescending grace of Jesus! As the Father loved him who was most worthy, he loved them who were most unworthy. The Father loved him as his Son and he loves them as his children.

"The Father gave all things into his hands;" so with himself, he freely gives us all things. The Father dearly appreciated him as Mediator, as responsible head of the Church, and the chief trustee of divine grace and gracious favor; which he had not for himself only, but for the direct benefit of those for whom he was willingly given appropriate custody of.

And he says, "I have been a faithful trustee. As the Father has committed his love to me, so I transmit it to you."

b) <u>The proofs and products of his love</u>: Christ loved his disciples, for he laid down his life for them. Others have laid down their lives, in content that their lives should be taken from them but Christ gave up his life; was not merely passive, but made it his own act and deed.

c) <u>The communication of his mind to the disciples</u>: **"All things that I have heard of my Father I have made known unto you."** As the secret wills of God, there are many things which we must be content not to know; but as to the revealed will of God, Jesus Christ has faithfully handed to us what he received of the Father.

Christ loved his disciples, for he chose and ordained them to be the prime instruments of his glory and honor in the world according to verse 16 of the context (see John chapter 15).

3. The Disciples' Love for Christ:

a) <u>It is to be a continuous love</u>: **"Continue in your love to me and in mine to you."** All that love Christ should continue faithfully in their genuine love to him. That is, to be always loving him and carefully taking all occasions to abundantly show it and to dearly love to the glorious end. We must carefully place our radiant happiness in the continuance of Christ's unconditional love for us. And naturally, make it our direct business to willingly give continued proofs of our love to Christ. That nothing may tempt us, to voluntarily withdraw from him, or naturally provoke him to withdraw from us.

b) <u>It is precisely a joyous love</u>: The familiar phrase, **"That my joy might remain in you."** Graciously granting to verse 11 of the context (see John chapter 15); the verse means not only that you might be full of joy; but that your joy in Christ and in his love may raise higher and higher until it comes to divine perfection, when "ye enter into the joy of the Lord." It is a dwelling place at home in Christ's abiding love; as in a resting place, at comparative ease in Christ's unconditional love; as a strong-hold, private safe in God's eternal love.

CHAPTER 3

THEREFORE, REPENT:

AUTHENTIC CHANGE

"And he came into all the country about Jordan, preaching the baptism of repentance for the remission of sins: As it is written in the book of the words of Isaiah the prophet, saying, the voice of one crying in the wilderness, Prepare ye the way of the Lord, make his paths straight. Every valley shall be filled. And every mountain and hill shall be brought low; and the crooked shall be made straight, and the rough ways shall be made smooth; and all flesh shall see the salvation of God" (Luke 3:3-6; KJV).

3. THE BELIEVER'S REPOSITION — YOU MUST CHANGE YOUR POSITION:

To marvelously become like Jesus, we must fill our lives with his infallible Word. We must voluntarily change from:

a) Living Life Without God — To Living Life With God (leave the old nature behind and begin with a fresh start)

<u>Questions for a Remarkable Transformation</u>:

- Ask yourself: Why is this necessary preparation for the believers?
- Are you indifferent about your present position? What is your attitude?

Once you have changed, this is the first step to becoming one with God. To change your moral position successfully, you have to properly understand yourself (spirit man). Ideally, you will genuinely need to turn from life without God to life with him. This sincerely means you mutually recognize your life without God is wrong; also to be sorry for the unspeakable pain caused by having an evil or immoral nature and to change to God's lovely way of living. Therefore, sincere repentance is how we show abiding faith in Jesus Christ.

To learn how to heartily repent and graciously receive divine forgiveness, faithfully follow these four reasonable steps below:

Step 1: YOU MUST BE GODLY SORRY

The first necessary step of sincere repentance is to instantly recognize you have committed a sin against God. You must genuinely feel true god-fearing sorry for what you have done badly and for willfully disobeying God. This includes feeling sincere sorry for any highly rated pain you may have cause toward other dear people.

In Second Corinthians 7:10 correctly says,

"For godly sorrow worketh repentance to salvation not to be repented of (means don't be sorry for feeling that way): but the sorrow of the world worketh death."

Step 2: CONFESS YOUR SIN TO GOD

There is a simple test to know precisely if you have sincerely repented of your mortal sins. If you humbly confess them and forsake them, then you have heartily repented.

In First John 1:9 speaks,

"If we confess our sins, he is faithful and just to forgive us our sins, and to cleanse us from all unrighteousness."

Step 3: ASK GOD FOR FORGIVENESS

If you have sinned mortally, you must sincerely ask for divine forgiveness. This could properly include a precise number of dear people. You must humbly ask God, anyone you have justly offended in any way, as private well as yourself for genuine forgiveness. You must also forgive others for intentionally hurting you.

In Matthew 6:14, 15 say,

"For if ye forgive men their trespasses, your heavenly Father will also forgive you: But if ye forgive not men their trespasses, neither will your Father forgive your trespasses."

You willingly see, in the glorious end; you must generously forgive yourself and undoubtedly know that God has forgiven you, even though you have sinned grievously.

Step 4: FORSAKE ALL YOUR SINS

Turn away from sin and never repeat the mortal sin. You will naturally see many are willing to humbly confess their mortal sins, at least after a hearty fashion. But few are willing to forsake them.

In the Book of Proverbs 28:13 says knowingly,

"He that covereth his sins shall not prosper: but whoso confesseth and forsaketh them shall have mercy."

As a remarkable result of which, directly preceding the successful introduction of Christ came John the Baptist, shouting fiercely in the savage wilderness. John's divine message was humble yourself, openly confess your mortal sins and heartily repent, graciously receive baptism. And open the way for the Messiah to take permanent hold of your dear lives. John's welcome announcement of the Messiah's coming fell softly on no one's attentive ears. He certainly didn't try leading his willing listeners into sincerely believing they could joyfully welcome the Savior with a mindless enthusiasm like that of a vulnerable child; who looks forward to a new toy for jolly Christmas. John's divine message was "Prepare ye the way of the Lord." To prepare refers to making something ready; way could also be translated road. In this way, a key part of preparing the way is to make his well-worn path straight.

When a mighty king proposed to tour a key part of his modern kingdoms in the east; he instantly sent a faithful messenger before him to promptly tell the dear people to diligently prepare the roads. So, John is universally regarded as the chosen messenger of the King. But necessary preparation on which he steadfastly insisted was preparation of humble heart and dear life.

He carefully said, "The King is coming, mend, not your roads, but your dear life."

Every willing person in the dear world has in common the humble duty to carefully make life fit for the King to see. The willingly people of Israel, who came to see this inspired prophet in the protected wilderness, were typically faced with a life-changing message. If they would prepare themselves, clear away the spiritual debris and straighten any crooked immoral paths; the way would be ready for their King and Messiah to come.

The Messiah that John the Baptist announced triumphantly is certainly a potential threat to anyone, who has become self-satisfied, and overly comfortable with their lives, values, and opinions? The King that John called people to diligently prepare for was the One who came to interrupt eagerly that normal course of modern life; to properly introduce the way of God. The glorified Christ was coming, and the people genuinely needed to be adequately prepared to meet him; even though the necessary preparation was going to disrupt their dear lives.

Which instantly reminds me of an evangelical story; two young men once opened an Automotive Detailing Shop and prospered economically. Then a famed evangelist came to their precious hometown, and one of them was miraculously saved. He tried diligently with great enthusiasm to gently persuade his managing partner to candidly confess his mortal sins. And willingly accept Salvation through our dear Lord and Savior Jesus Christ also but to no avail.

"Why won't you?" humbly asked the born-again man.

Listen, smilingly; the other man said politely, "If I humbly confess my mortal sins and get saved too. Who's going to clean the cars?"

John, the Baptist, says eagerly we have to prepare the way for Christ. If you had an important guest coming for a delightful dinner, what would you do? Whenever we have special guests coming to our dear house, Wanda, Tommy and I always clean up inside the house. There are so many remarkable things to do when preparing for honored guests: diligently prepare a special meal; pick-up toys off of the floors; gaily decorate with some lovely flowers; carefully light the good smelling candles; voluntarily put on nice clothes and properly fix our glossy hair, and so on.

However, in my case, the significant and major preparation I do to carefully prepare for honored guests is to spotlessly clean certain key areas of the house; especially the communal bathrooms. I get rid of junk just lying around the house. In other kind words, ethnically cleansing the inside of your lovely house is genuine repentance.

What will you do if you have a very special guest coming? What is the most urgent thing you genuinely need to do to adequately prepare for the coming Christ? Truly, we celebrate with our special guests. We heartily enjoy one another and willingly share a delicious meal. We share in common God's passionate love and divine grace with dear family, beloved friends, and kind neighbors. However, I sincerely believe we should. As John, the Baptist proclaimed, get cleaned up inside. And gratefully recognize our sinful nature, in one kind word, sincere repentance. This is the first and most urgent thing to do, to go to eternal heaven.

In this sacred scripture, John says gently we need to voluntarily stop and take the time to carefully examine ourselves. Are there specific areas in our dear lives that are in need of sincere repentance? Are there personal activities that we are naturally involved in that lead others or us to unhealthy living? Are there meaningful relationships that are in specific need of necessary repair or more valuable time and devoted attention? Do we willingly give ourselves over to God for God's divine purposes? John dearly wants us to heartily repent, so that we can receive divine forgiveness and 'see the eternal salvation of God (see verse 6 of Luke 3).

The Bible naturally says in Acts 17:30,

"And the time of this ignorance God winked at (meaning overlook); but now commandeth all men every where to repent."

What is genuine repentance? What does a person do when he or she sincerely repents? The English word 'repentance' comes from two Latin words, which means to be sorry again. Repentance is obediently turning from mortal sin; an act of the conscious will whereby one resolves, by the divine help of God to voluntarily give up his sins; a change of willing mind with sincere respect to sin that leads to a change of behavior. Repentance means turning away from all sin. Some dear people are willing to give up all their mortal sins except the one sin that is dearest to their dear hearts.

Jesus said willfully,

"Of any man will come after me, let him deny himself, and take up his cross, and follow me" (Matthew 16:24).

The sacred word of God has much to say about genuine repentance. All of the great preachers of both the Old and New Testament gave repentance a central place in their messages. The prophets of Old urged the people of Israel to repent of their sins and turn to God. When Peter preached to the mighty multitude on the glorious day of Pentecost, and many were instantly converted and cried out, "Men and brethren, what shall we do?

Peter said unto them, "Repent, and be baptized every one of you in the name of Jesus Christ."

Sincere repentance is so important that God commands "all men everywhere to repent." It is a message that is greatly needed today. Willing men and women have conveniently forgotten God and given themselves over to sin. As they traditionally group in the eternal darkness which has settled over the earth and cry out "what shall we do?" If they will but listen, they will naturally hear that call of God which came to men of old, "repent of your sins."

In the book of Revelation, chapters 2 and 3, our dear Lord promptly sent seven straightforward letters to seven local churches. He called upon five of the seven to repent. The church at Ephesus was to repent because she left her first love. The church at Pergamum (or Pergamos) as was to repent because she allowed the doctrine of Balaam to be taught and to eat things sacrificed unto idols and to commit living in sin. The church at Thyatira was to repent because she suffered Jezebel to teach and seduce God's servants to commit sin.

The church at Sardis was to repent because she was a dying congregation. And the church at Laodicea was to repent because she thought she was rich and did not need anything, but God said she needed everything:

- She said we are rich; God said she was poor.
- She said gaily we are wealthy; God said gently she was a wretched.
- She said we are busy in the faithful church; God said gratefully she was miserable.
- She said we naturally have a lovely vision; God said earnestly she was blind.
- She said we are properly dressed in fine clothes; God said sympathetically she was naked.
- She said we are abundantly satisfied; God said she genuinely made him sick.

In her private opinion, she had typically arrived; she had undoubtedly reached her intended destination. She did not know that she was neither hot nor cold, but lukewarm, and God was ready to allegedly spit her out of his mouth. The dear Lord called upon these five local churches to sincerely repent or else he would voluntarily remove their candlestick and they would instantly cease to be a dazzling light in deepening darkness.

Paul speaks enthusiastically of this genuine repentance as being precisely toward God. It is toward God because all sin is against God. A man cannot repent of his sins until he naturally sees them in their proper relation to a holy God. We sometimes speak of a man as sinning against himself or sinning against his fellow man. But we do not see sin as it really is until we realize that it is something against God.

David had sinned grievously against his fellow man. He had taken Uriah's beloved wife and had instantly brought about the death of Uriah in order to cover up his sin, but when he came willingly to see his sin in its true light.

He cried out to God, "Against thee; thee only, have I sinned and done this evil in thy sight."

No man repents of his sins until he is convicted of his sins. And until he becomes deeply conscious that he is wrong and is a sinner in the precious sight of a Holy God. This unshakable conviction is the mighty work of the Holy Spirit.

Jesus spoke passionately about the coming of the Holy Spirit, and said politely,

"And when he is come, he will reprove the world of sin, and of righteousness, and of judgment" (St. John 16:8; KJV).

Meaning that the Holy Spirit would demonstrate peacefully the eternal truth of Christ beyond the genuine fear of contradiction; the Holy Spirit convicts unbelievers through believers who witness about Christ (typically see John 15:26, 27). Faithful believers are the official mouthpiece for God's mighty voice. The precious content of the faithful witness that the Spirit powerfully reinforces includes the eternal truth about sin, righteousness, and judgment. The various temptations we are experiencing are normal, and all believers throughout the ages have had to resist temptation. God is so good that he will not allow you to typically experience anything for which he has not prepared you to stand obediently. He will give every faithful believer the divine grace and power to willingly endure. When Christ was tempted by the clever devil, he steadfastly resisted until the devil went away (see precisely Matthew 4:1–11); and graciously according to the Book of James, he enthusiastically encouraged us to do the same (see James 4:7). Successful resistance begins by bathing our conscious minds with the divine Word of God and standing our moral ground. We have in common the fulfilled promise; after all, that the irresistible temptations we typically experience will never go beyond the common experiences of others, or beyond our remarkable ability to deal carefully with them (naturally see First Corinthians 10:13).

In First John 3:4 and 9 of the well-worn Holy Bible declare willingly,

"Whosoever committeth sin transgresseth also the law: for sin is the transgression of the law.

And verse 9 states devotedly in First John chapter 3,

"Whosoever is born of God doth not commit sin; for his seed remaineth in him: and he cannot sin, because he is born of God."

What is a sin? In carefully considering the direct question of mortal sin, we are typically faced with two startling facts.

The first established fact is that man makes so little of sin. To some, it is a convincing illusion, a religious mirage, the clever invention of some fanatic. It is steadfastly denied, joked about and laughed merrily at by the man. Many, who sincerely believe sin to remain a remarkable fact, continue earnestly in it with little conscious thought of its proper penalty.

The second established fact is that God makes so much of mortal sin.

God said succinctly, granting to Ezekiel 18:20,

"The soul that sinneth, it shall die."

In Romans 6:23, Paul says enthusiastically,

"The wages of sin is death."

In Proverbs 6:16-19, the inspired poet speaks authoritatively,

"These six things doth the Lord hate: yea, seven are an abomination unto him: a proud look, a lying tongue, and hands that shed innocent blood, an heart that deviseth wicked imaginations, feet that be swift in running to mischief, a false witness that speaketh lies, and he that soweth discord among brethren."

And Moses said earnestly, in Deuteronomy 25:16 that,

"All that do unrighteous are an abomination unto the Lord."

Mortal sin is precisely an evil force. Its overwhelming presence cannot be escaped in this dear life, but it can be overcome by the divine power of God. It is impossible to deny the existence of sin when the whole world is in a conflict between good and evil. If sin were not a fact, there would be no crime; we would not need jails or prisons. We would need no locks on our doors or vaults for our valuables.

(Sin Review): What is a sin?

- To some sin is being indiscreet, or it is a weakness of the flesh.
- To others, it is the absence from good.
- To the so–called scholar, sin is ignorance. And to the evolutionist, it is the aggressive nature of the filthy beast. The latest theory is that sin is a terrible disease to be properly treated by modern science because man is not a miserable sinner, he is only sick.
- To others, sin is precisely an active form of personal selfishness. But God instantly declares that sin is naturally an immoral transgression of the divine law.

Granting First John 3:4, this read attentively,

"Whosoever committeth sin transgresseth also the law: for sin is the transgression of the law."

- Sin is precisely a personal rebellion against God (see Isaiah 1:2).
- Sin is unbelief; it makes God a terrible liar. God who cannot lie said, **"All have sinned;"** all naturally includes you and me. We have sinned grievously against God by foolish thoughts, terrible words, and shameful deeds. We have involuntarily committed terrible sins of commission and sins of omission.
- Sin is merely going your careless way, allegedly planning your life according to your own will, without diligently seeking the mighty will of God (see Isaiah 53:6). When we sin grievously, we should always remember (never forget):

1. Always remember to expect the unexpected:

- Sin is precisely foolishness, an incredible folly to intentionally deceive you; an overwhelming force to merely destroy you and a notorious fact to bitterly condemn you; sin is a volitional act of disobedience against the revealed will of God.

In the Epistle to the victorious Romans, Paul carefully takes in the office of extolling and explaining the personal nature of mortal sin. Sin naturally includes devastating consequences of which we dearly need to be aware of its miserable wages. As the Book of Romans points out, sin enslaves willingly people and demands that they obey its lustfulness (see victorious Romans 6:6, verses 12 and 20). "To sin is to fall short of the divine glory of God (see victorious Romans 3:23)." And when you sin, you merely live a miserable life without God. You are trapped in sins and cannot live up to the holy lifestyle that God undoubtedly intended when he created you.

The well-worn Bible abundantly illustrates that as faithful Christians we willingly died to sin when we properly identified with Christ in genuine faith; so, don't you see, we have been gently freed from the everlasting dominion of mortal sin to live an active life of faithful obedience to God? Paul thoughtfully said a believer who continues bitterly in sin would be positively denying his or her own identity in Christ.

Jesus carefully closed a compelling argument with Nicodemus by telling him:

*"Except a man be born again,
he cannot see the Kingdom of God" (John 3:3; KJV).*

Being naturally born again is a spiritual birth. It is as much of a miraculous birth as the natural birth; it is not only just a figure of speech but also a commitment to God. Birth has two sides: one side has to do with the seed of man, and the other side has to do with the precious seed of God.

Willingly granting to First Peter 1:23, which says heartily:

*"Being born, not of corruptible seed, but of incorruptible, by
the word of God, which liveth and abideth for ever:"*

1. A corruptible seed naturally produces a corruptible nature. A corruptible man can naturally produce only a corruptible seed. Granting Matthew 7:18; Jesus justly said, **"A good tree cannot bring forth evil fruit; neither can a corrupt tree bring forth good fruit."** Plus victorious Romans 3:23 naturally says, **"For all have sinned and come short of the glory of God."** Because everyone who is naturally born in the creative world is born in sin. Therefore, we are not sinners because we sin grievously; we sin grievously because we are sinners.

2. An incorruptible seed produces an incorruptible nature. Graciously according to Second Peter 1:4, which say thoughtfully: **"Whereby are given unto us exceeding great and precious promises: that by these ye might be partakers of the nature, having escaped the corruption that is in the world through lust."** You cannot corrupt that which is incorruptible. Therefore, the

incorruptible seed of God issues a new nature that cannot be corrupted at any time, or in any way. Being born again produces the life of Christ, and this life is made living in man by the indwelling of the Holy Spirit; therefore, you cannot become a child of God by joining the church, any more than a monkey could become a man by joining the human race. He may act wisely like a man, dress like a man and may naturally try to live peacefully like a man but he would still be a monkey. Now, if by some divine miracle, the monkey could be born again of the precious seed of man. Only then could he naturally become a man. As a direct result, the only way to naturally become a beloved child of God is to be naturally born from above by the incorruptible seed of God.

In the above-mentioned Bible scripture (John 3:3); we willingly see Jesus and Nicodemus face to face, Jesus the Son of God and Nicodemus the dear son of natural man. Nicodemus was precisely a very religious man, but he was not a child of God.

"Hmm, what a shock it must have been precisely to learn that his religion was not enough."

"And little do you know it never is."

He came willingly to Jesus, carefully addressing Him as a beloved teacher come from God. Jesus precisely knew Nicodemus, as he knows all men, and Jesus knew that: he needed more than a beloved teacher he naturally needed a divine Saviour. And he needed more than religion he needed regeneration; and he needed more than ceremonial law he needed an eternal life.

Jesus promptly began by going right to the key point when he said humbly, "Ye must be born again."

Since faithful believers have willingly died with Christ and have also been raised with Him, Paul now urges sincere Christians

71

to carefully consider themselves dead to sin. Although, before successful conversion, we were still enslaved to the terrible power of mortal sin; right now we are free to steadfastly resist it.

It's time for you to get with those who have your answers and get away from those who have your problems. Stop politely telling God how big your problems are and start telling your problems how big your God is. In a welcome addition, humbly asks God to naturally make your dear life a sacred image for His glowing light. To shine gloriously through you like a flexible mirror to faithfully reflect him.

Humbly pray with me this earnest prayer (a prayer I wrote for my dear mother):

Dear GOD, my Father in merciful heaven, generously forgive me of all my mortal sins. Carefully save me and instantly show me the correct way that I may not be lost. I sincerely believe that Jesus your Son, died for my worldly sins, rose for my precious liberty. And now that I am miraculously saved, I sincerely thank you God for willingly allowing me to grow with all your might and main in you. So that you may live humbly with me, precious moment by moment, glorious day by day, and peaceful night by night. On the precious, holy name of Jesus, I do humbly pray. Amen.

Now, let us prepare ourselves for the celebration of the coming of Jesus Christ through repentance. Judge ourselves!

Repent of any sin:

- God has no hands, but our hands to do His work today.
- God has no feet, but our feet to lead men to His paths of righteousness.
- God has no help, but our help to lead sinners to His side.
- God has no tongue, but our tongue to tell men that Christ, hung, bled, and died; but early that third day morning, He rose with victory and power!!!

*"Looking unto Jesus the author and finisher of our faith;
who for the joy that was set before him endured the cross,
despising the shame, and is set down at the right hand of the
throne of God" (Hebrews 12:2; KJV).*

What this means is that we need to focus consistently on Christ instead of our own circumstances; looking here means fixing one's eyes trustingly. Christ has done everything necessary for us to endure in our faith. He is our example and model, for he focused on the joy that was set before him. His attention was not on the agonies of the Cross, but on the crown; not on the suffering, but the reward. Jesus is now at the right hand of the Father's throne, waiting for his enthronement on his throne (see Revelation 3:21).

The Judgment of the Nations

At this divine judgment, the King willingly gives the heavenly kingdom to those who have eternal life. This divine judgment is not a judgment of the great white throne (typically see Revelation 20:11–15). An accurate comparison of the two divine judgments will properly establish the following facts further down:

1. The divine judgment of the mighty nations will naturally take place when the Son of man shall come in his glory, then shall he sit upon the eternal throne of his divine glory.

2. At this judgment, he will judge the living nations (see Joel 3:11—16; OT). At the white throne judgment, he will judge the wicked dead.

3. At this judgment, there will be no resurrection of the dead. At the great white throne, all the wicked dead are raised; "the sea gave up the dead which were in it; and death and hell delivered up the dead which were in them" (Revelation 20:13).

4. At this judgment, the judge is God the King judging the living nations in his earthly kingdom. At the great white throne, the judge is God, judging only the wicked dead.

5. At this judgment, there are no books opened. At the great white throne, the books were opened.

6. At this judgment, there are three classes judged. They are:

   a. Sheep— the saved (see Revelation 7:9–17).
   b. Goats— the unsaved (see 11 Thessalonians 1:7–10).
   c. Brethren— the elect of Israel (see Revelation 7:1–8; also Romans 11:25–28).

The Great White Throne Judgment

At this divine judgment, there are no saved and no mighty kingdoms. They are all cast into the burning lake of fire. There is only one class:

a. The unknown dead (unbelievers).

The Great White Throne Judgment, note the following facts below:

1. At this divine judgment, the wicked dead will desperately seek a hiding place from the radiant face of the Lord Jesus Christ, the infallible judge. But there is no hiding place.

2. At this divine judgment, the unknown dead (unfortunate ones), small and great will stand before God. But the greatness of the great will be of no value. "There is none that doeth good, no not one" (Romans 3:12).

3. At this divine judgment, the sacred book of eternal life will be carefully opened. Why the book of life if there is

no saved at this judgment? The wicked will be shown that God in his mercy provided space for them in the book of life, so that they are without excuse (see Romans 1:18–20).

4. At this divine judgment, the unknown dead (unfortunate ones) will be judged according to their personal works. God is a just God, and since there are degrees of punishment in hell, some will be punished more than others (see Luke 12:42–48).

5. At this divine judgment, there will be no acquittal, no higher court to which the lost may appeal. It is lost and lost forever. It is damned to all eternity and that is precisely without eternal hope. There is a burning hell (typically see Luke 16:19–31), and in hell, there is no reasonable hope, no heartfelt sympathy, no sincere love; even the unconditional love of God does not extend beyond the secure portals of eternal hell.

In the present circumstances, willingly let us notice underneath:

The Crown of Righteousness

"Henceforth there is laid up for me a crown of righteousness, which the Lord, the righteous judge, shall give me at that day: and not to me only, but unto all them also that love his appearing" (11 Timothy 4:8; KJV).

The crown of righteousness is a reward, but it is not to be confused with the righteousness of God. Which a person receives when they enter into Christianity or perhaps when they become a child of God.

"For at that time, that person is made the righteousness of God in him."

This saving righteousness is a gift to be accepted by the lost. The crown of righteousness is a reward to be earned by a child of God (meaning a person that is saved). If a child of God carefully looks for and genuinely loves the divine doctrine of the Second Coming of Christ, it will powerfully affect his whole lifestyle. Look at the dynamic impact the Word of God had on the life of the apostle Paul. He understood the eternal potential of a lifetime of faithful service to Jesus Christ. Who would return with rewards for those who stick it out over the long haul?

The crown of righteousness is a special reward given to those who serve God faithfully on this earth (see Matthew 5:10–12). There will be as many crowns as there are runners who finish the race well. All who have loved his appearing are those believers in Christ who have lived faithfully in the hope of his return. We must faithfully have the Spirit of Christ. We must be willing to meet dear people where they are naturally. And carefully assist them where they dearly need to be religiously. Willingly giving every precious bit of the divine glory to God, altogether the everlasting honor and the genuine praise. For too long we have been doing just enough to get by. Noticeable time has long since past where anything will do. God is properly calling for some bold preachers to willingly take an uncompromising stand in this crooked society.

The sacred scripture says sympathetically according to Acts 18:9-10:

"Then spake the Lord to Paul in the night by a vision, Be not afraid, but speak, and hold not thy peace."

Verse 10,

"For I am with thee and no man shall set on thee to hurt thee: for I have much people in this city."

First, as you can typically see Second Timothy 2:15 speaks authoritatively with a direct command. This wisely says,

"Study to show thyself approved unto God, a workman that needeth not to be ashamed, rightly dividing the word of truth."

This is most essential: an engaged workman of the well-worn Bible should make every effort to properly handle the inspired word of God accurately. Failure to do so will naturally lead to divine judgment (typically see James 3:1). It is imperative to know that courageous bold preachers are dearly needed in this sinful society. There is precisely nothing in a modern society like a well equipped preacher.

The dear Lord said sympathetically to this modern preacher of the sacred text. And to all the willing others of us; whom he rightfully has called, willingly chosen and dutifully sent, "Don't be afraid."

Have no fear but speak and do not keep silent; for I am with you and no one is going to harm you. That is "if" we do what he tells us? Only then is he responsible for sustaining us.

The Bible history divinely reveals that Paul the Apostle had been in Antioch and now moved to Corinth. Therefore, Corinth was undoubtedly a unique and very worldly city. Because of its precise location, the capital city was full of local people like successful gamblers, prostitutes and drug dealers.

Countless people went willingly through Corinth to go north and they went through Corinth to go west. Corinth was a very cosmopolitan city due to their overseas shipping and transport industry. There were aggressively local people of all races and all income levels. Some local laborers were just making ends meet.

Let me politely show you what I sincerely mean. In economic reality, people are naturally making more money now than they have ever made in life's modern history, not because of a gradual increase in salary. But because they are working long and hard hours just to make ends properly meet. Instantly notice the first remarkable thing Paul did when he came into Corinth; he found a job. He got together with Aquila and Pricilla they worked diligently on used tents and ministered in a magnificent church that willingly met in their lovely house. Paul never complained about money, but we know what a strain financial stress can be on our life.

I sincerely believe when Paul had arrived in Corinth he was discouraged and worn out. Paul had been in local prison, stoned, and intentionally left for dead; forcibly brought before selected judges, and experienced abuse of all terrible kinds. So, therefore, these horrible things can naturally wear on you after awhile.

Paul may have been physically weary. Notice in graceful (verse 9) God speaks convincingly to Paul. He willingly tells him not to be afraid and don't stop preaching. I think strategically this authoritative command instantly gives us a moral sense of feeling to the undeniable fact that Paul was weary. Afraid of more uncompromising hostilities and he was discouraged:

- If you willingly give your dear heart to something and it doesn't go as well as you planed, it is easy to be discouraged.
- If you carefully put precious hours into preparing for something and no one shows up, it is discouraging.
- If you are tremendously excited about a particular program but no one shares your breathless excitement, it is discouraging.
- If you look forward to a big event but it doesn't go as you had properly planned, it is easy to be discouraged.

When we are discouraged, we naturally tend to instantaneously draw false conclusions. We sincerely believe we are a failure. We may feel that we are obviously the wrong person for the job. We instantly wonder, what is wrong with me? We become confused, embarrassed, and defeated. Discouraged people are physically drained of sad life and tireless energy.

There are precisely four remarkable things God said confidently to Paul, and they are respectfully:

1. **"Do Not Be Afraid."** This is one of the most common commands in the sacred Scripture. Seventy-nine precious times in the well-worn Bible there are commands to not be afraid. So, let me be honest with you. Concentrated

most of the time we are particularly un-helped by those who say wistfully, "Don't worry" or "don't be afraid." The words seem hollow and empty. When other people say this to us we sincerely believe they don't understand the possible situation. If they undoubtedly did, they would naturally worry and be afraid too!

But it's different when God heartily says these precise words. When God voluntarily tells us not to worry he is saying, "Don't worry because I'm going to take care of your needs." In others words, he wants us to trust him; he sincerely wants us to instantly find our needed strength in him. He gently reminds us in Proverbs 3:5, 6: "**Trust in the Lord with all thine heart; and lean not unto thine own understanding. In all thy ways acknowledge him, and he shall direct thy paths**."

Also, when God says enthusiastically, "Don't be afraid," he is instantly telling us that he will carefully protect us.

2. **"Keep On Speaking, Do Not Be Silent."** God politely tells Paul not to give up. I naturally think it is interesting that even though Paul was discouraged he faithfully kept doing what he was supposed to do. He continued to speak enthusiastically and reason in the local synagogue. He was obedient even when his wounded heart wasn't fully in the glorious work. Paul remained faithful even when he naturally felt like quitting.

3. **"I Am With You, No One Will Harm You."** These are undoubtedly great words. We can typically face anything if God is by our side. When we are walking humbly with God, we are safe, even if we are merely preaching to wicked folks that don't like us. God has promised faithfully he is using every situation for his divine purpose. We are safe in his almighty hands.

4. **"You Are Not Alone, As You Think."** God told Paul that there were many of his dear people in this capital city. We must remember the dear Lord provides for his chosen people. If we are willingly chosen by God, graciously according to divine call. In Bible-Scriptures, Matthew 20 and the second part of verse 16; 22:14. Both verses articulate, **"For many are called, but few chosen."**

In unique essence, this faithfully represents an unfortunate rural boy growing up in the southern hills of Arkansas; where we gently raised free-range chickens in our backyard. And for this sentimental reason, I am instantly reminded of an authentic story with direct reference to my dear mother; as she was about to make a delicious meal for the family table. Once a week the precious day came around where mamma would step out through the back door, into the chickens' patch; where the organic chickens ran free; roaming here and there, and perhaps some of everywhere in the fruitful garden.

So, there carefully laid a big brown bag of yellow corn feed at the back door; mamma would frantically grab a hand full of corn seeds and then she would naturally make the insistent call: Here chick, chick, chick! Here a chick, chick, chick! Here a chick, chick, chick! The free-range chickens would voluntarily stop whatever they were doing and came running to answer eagerly her call. They would eat heartily from the rosy palm of her left hand. And then she would instantly catch one in her right arm. And if it was not big enough, she would wisely let it go free. Dear mamma, kept on repeating gently the proper actions until she undoubtedly found one big enough and that was suitable for the dinner table. And then she would naturally take it to the successful kill.

So, therefore, many are rightfully called but only a few carefully chosen:

- Judas was naturally called, but he was not among the chosen.
- Saul was rightfully called, but he was not among the chosen.
- Ananias and Saphira were promptly called, but they were not among the chosen.

You naturally see, "For many are undoubtedly called." In other words, everyone is called, but some people refuse the invitation. They refuse to obey the Gospel of Jesus Christ and are not chosen. Even all who merely hear the glorious gospel, whether local Jews or Gentiles; but only a few are carefully chosen, only those who willingly obey the Gospel of Jesus Christ.

In Romans 1:6 it says thoughtfully, "**You are among those who have been called to belong to Jesus Christ**." Every person who is saved has been called of the Lord from something to something.

The fact encourages me that Paul became discouraged. I am naturally encouraged because it typically means I am not alone in being overwhelmed on rare occasion. Throughout the well-worn Bible, you will instantly see many of God's chosen people were discouraged:

- David was discouraged, and Elijah was discouraged.
- Think carefully about it. Don't you think there were dreadful days when Noah wanted to stop building the Ark?
- Surely there were days wandering in the dreary wilderness when Moses and Aaron wanted to say bitterly, "We quit!"
- Do you really think Ezekiel and Jeremiah were always thrilled about their odd jobs?
- Do you think the beloved disciples were never discouraged at the lack of overwhelming response from the wicked people?

When all is said and done, according to the Old Testament, Deuteronomy 7:9:

"Know therefore, that the Lord thy God, he is God, the faithful God, the only true God, which keepeth covenant and mercy with them that love him and keep his commandments to a thousand generations."

God, being who he is, cannot cease to be precisely what he is. And being what he is, he cannot act out of divine character with himself. He is precisely a faithful God. We know by heart God's greatest act of faithfulness was to voluntarily send the Messiah (Jesus). And speaking of faithfulness, Jesus Christ was prophesied to be a faithful priest, according to (see 1 Samuel 2:35).

In modern Hebrews, chapter 2, the prolific writer says enthusiastically,

"He was the faithful high priest in things pertaining to God, to make reconciliation for the sins of the people"
(Verse 17).

Therefore, Revelation 19 accurately describes his glorious return, properly calling him faithful and true. Christ was precisely, and is, and is to be faithful. My Christian friend, we willingly serve a faithful and true God. It is imperative we understand there were a new generation and a new time; a time to gratefully receive the precious promise, to move forward, to properly complete what the older generation had begun humbly.

In graceful verse 9 (Deuteronomy 7) says thoughtfully,

"Know therefore that the Lord thy God, he is God, the faithful God."

Throughout all precious times, God has remained true to his heartfelt commitment made to Abraham, Isaac, and Jacob. He is precisely a faithful God. The latter part of this sacred verse says gently,

"Love Him and keep His commandments to a thousand generations."

Loving God always finds joyous expression in doing his will. God willingly took Israel out of Egypt partly because of his genuine love for them. And partly because he had naturally made promises to Abraham, Isaac, and Jacob and he was faithfully keeping these promises.

God said according to John 14:15,

"Of you love me, keep my commandments."

The dear Lord is a God of divine justice. He will amply repay those who rebel against him. Willingly let me pulse for a precious moment and humbly ask this hypothetical question. Why does God dearly love us? Now Moses properly addresses the direct issue of God's genuine love and faithfulness. Many people struggle, respectfully asking, "Why does God love me? What does he naturally see in me?"

I feel like there's nothing about me that God could genuinely love, so I reasonably question whether he really does or not."

To be perfectly truthful with you today, the real source of that peculiar kind of thinking is unconscious pride. The honest truth is God doesn't love us because of what is inside of us. He genuinely loves us because of what is inside of him. If you keep looking thoughtfully for something that God can find lovable about you, you will never find it. God sincerely loves you simply because he loves you, period. He loved us and miraculously saved us, not because of who we were or are naturally (underneath see Titus 3).

Paul gently reminded Titus in chapter 3 that God undoubtedly saved us,

"Not by works of righteousness which we have done, but according to his mercy he saved us, by the washing of regeneration, and renewing of the Holy Ghost; which he shed on us abundantly through Jesus Christ our Saviour; that being justified by his grace, we should be made heirs according to the hope of eternal life" (Verses 5, 6 and 7).

Many devout Christians are intentionally trying to work diligently out their self-esteem issues, to undoubtedly discover what is so lovable about them. But they are looking wistfully in the wrong place. Yes, they naturally need to carefully look at how loving God is, rather than how lovable they are. Our sacred scripture politely tell us a lot about the loving nature of God.

It properly tells us that, God is faithful. That, "He is precisely God, the faithful God; that, he is God the merciful God." And he faithfully keeps, "His loving genuine kindness to a thousandth generation; because God is all these remarkable things." We dearly need to faithfully keep his divine commandments.

As we voluntarily enter the intercessory role, we will now learn considered God himself; in the absence of all outward spiritual fellowship, is undoubtedly a sufficing portion for eternal faith. And even in the familiar face of what looks like devastating defeat. In an undeniable sense, God's divine mercy cannot be exhausted, because it begins anew each and every glorious morning. In the Lamentations 3:22, 23 of the inspired prophet Jeremiah say sympathetically,

> *"It is of the Lord's mercies that we are not consumed, because his compassion fails not. They are new every morning: great is thy faithfulness."*

As well, we can be certain this will never change; because the Holy Spirit says triumphantly, "Great is your faithfulness."

This naturally reminds me of the familiar hymn, which says enthusiastically:

> *"Great is thy faithfulness. O God my Father, There is no shadow of turning with Thee; Thou changes not, Thy compassion, they fail not, as Thou hast been Thou forever wilt be. Faithfulness! Morning by morning new mercies I see; all I have needed Thy hand hath provided, great is Thy faithfulness, Lord unto me."*

Gratefully considered,

If We Will, Then God Will

"Of my people, which are called by my name, shall humble themselves, and pray, and seek my face, and turn from their wicked ways; then will I hear from heaven, and will forgive their sin, and will heal their land" (2 Chronicles 7:14).

Here as you well know, as you are reading carefully this remarkable passage of sacred scripture, this is a striking illustration of God's everlasting covenant with Solomon. He pleaded earnestly with God on behalf of the dear people and continued thoughtfully to sincerely pray with precise determination until the precious Lord carefully answered him. It's imperative to understand my Christian friend that God was speaking to Israel, as indicated by our text phrase above and below,

"Of my people, which are called by my name."

What this phrase means is that if we (you and I). Because when God speaks earnestly of his dear people, he is clearly not talking about any person who comes to his local church. He is speaking naturally about people set apart to him; the faithful believers, those who through faith in Christ have been awash in his precious blood. From this, we instantly become God's dear people, and he binds us to himself. When we become God's dear people, we become intimately bound to him. As a holy God, he naturally takes it upon himself to make sure we are holy and righteous.

Now, the word 'if' is typically used in this humorous verse as a function word to properly introduce a passionate exclamation politely expressing the primarily grammatical relationships.

"If my people, which are called by my name, shall humble themselves, and pray, and seek my face, and turn from their wicked ways; then will I hear from heaven, and will forgive their sin, and will heal their land."

This graceful verse, therefore, sets out the remarkable conditions of God's blessing on his dear people as a devoted whole. He properly called his dear people to humble themselves, to earnestly pray and humbly seek his beloved face. They were politely called to instantly turn from their wicked ways.

God said reassuringly in remarkable Revelation 2:5,

"Remember therefore from whence thou art fallen, and repent, and do the first works; or else I will come unto thee quickly, and will remove thy candlestick out of his place, except thou repent."

In other kind words, sincerely repent or its lights out! What this means in more precise detail is that, if God's dear people properly meaning those who are set apart to him would typically do four remarkable things. God would respond positively in three fantastic ways:

1. The dear Lord's precious people needed to become humble, that is confess. You can willingly share any wrongdoing with God and know he genuinely understands and still loves you. In brilliant First John 1:9 the dear Lord says sympathetically, **"If we confess our sins, he is faithful and just to forgive us our sins, and to cleanse us from all unrighteousness."**

2. They dearly needed to humbly pray or sincerely repent. What good is humble confession without sincere repentance? David is properly called by sacred Scripture, "A man after God's own heart." And one of the practical reasons for that is David knew how to sincerely pray. Sincere prayer is imperative. We are typically commanded to pray according to Luke 18:1: **"Men ought always to pray, and not to faint."** And Matthew 6:41 says thoughtfully, **"Watch and pray, that ye enter not into temptation: the spirit indeed is willing, but the flesh is weak."** Payer is talking earnestly and listening carefully to God, typically having social fellowship with God.

3. They dearly needed to diligently seek his beloved face; to properly find God is to have his face revealed to you, in your faithful heart, for God dwells fondly in a humble man (woman). Bible scripture Psalm 27:8 says reassuringly, **"When thou saidst, Seek ye my face; my heart said unto thee, Thy face, Lord, will I seek."**

4. They needed to turn or come back to God; when we carefully turn from our wicked ways, it uniquely qualifies us for eternal salvation, but it takes genuine faith in Christ to naturally acquire it. It is impossible to typically have saving faith and not repent. In Proverbs 28:13 say, **"He that covereth his sins shall not prosper: but whoso confesseth and forsaketh them shall have mercy."**

The prodigal son had a change of mind, and his change of mind affected a change of heart; and his change of heart affected a change of will. True repentance is a change of mind, heart, and will. Let us willingly take a closer look at the three ways in which God would respond to Israel's obedience:

1. "God would graciously hear from eternal heaven." The most important part of this phrase is that God is never so far away to hear us. If we come with the right mind and the right heart. All can be made well.

2. "God would generously forgive their mortal sin." We willingly take divine forgiveness for granted, and that is not right! Many of us are so cultured by the merciful provision of genuine forgiveness. That we cannot even think of what it would be like if God had not forgiven us in Christ. Our conscious pride and ungratefulness reach such heights that we even dare to justly complain that God is the likely criminal. When God passes judgment rather than naturally brings divine forgiveness. It is naturally this thinking that leads to what we now know as victim theology. It is not my fault I did something wrong; it is the other person's

fault. Forgiveness means that we are at fault. Jesus satisfactorily settled it so clearly in the dear Lord's Prayer when he told according to Matthew 6:12, "And forgive us our debts, as we forgive our debtors." God's dear people are rooted in everlasting mercy and divine forgiveness.

3. "God would miraculously heal their fertile land." The first eternal reward dealt faithfully with a completed restoration of direct communication. And the second eternal reward properly dealt with genuine forgiveness of moral debt. Now we naturally find this one to be a pleasant relief from various forms of chastisement. The fertile land is where we all live. The precious life has become hard in some way because we have sinned against the dear Lord. Do you merely remember when God willingly sent modern plagues upon Egypt to convincingly show his divine power? And persuade Pharaoh to gently free his dear people from modern slavery? Solomon has prominently mentioned some of these already. He prominently mentioned a land might suffer mightily from famine, earthquakes, mildew, flies, frogs, locust, grasshopper, sickness, or even an enemy threat. These created things can happen right where we live naturally. It is time that we diligently seek God's miraculous healing upon our dear lives. I sincerely want to promptly challenge you to carefully establish a true relationship, one with yourself and one with God that you will heartily repent of any sin in your life. And actively seek the radiant face of God so that you can typically experience remarkable growth and the true power of God in your life!

Growing In Grace

The well-worn Bible says heartily in Ephesians 4:32,

"We need to be kind one to another, tenderhearted, forgiving one another as God through Christ had forgiven us."

And graceful verses 22 through 24 of that same chapter say this:

"That ye put off concerning the former conversation the old man, which is corrupt according to the deceitful lusts; And be renewed in the spirit of your mind; And that ye put on the new man, which after God is created in righteousness and true holiness."

Now, in this particular verse, Paul carefully compared the Christian life to stripping off the dirty clothes of a sinful past and willingly putting on the new clothes of Christ's eternal righteousness. Looking eagerly at Second Peter 3:18,

"But grow in grace, and in the knowledge of our Lord and Savior Jesus Christ. To him be glory both now and forever. Amen."

In this graceful verse, Peter precisely reveals four grand stages of spiritual growth in the Christian life:

1. The Baby Stage:

Typically see First Corinthians 3:1-4 say carefully,

"And I, brethren, could not speak unto you as unto spiritual, but as unto carnal, even as unto babes in Christ. I have fed you with milk, and not with meat: for hitherto (up to this time) ye were not able to bear it, neither yet now are ye able. For ye are yet carnal: for whereas there is among you envying, and strife, and divisions, are ye not carnal, and walk as men? For while one saith, I am of Paul; and another, I am of A-pol'-los; are ye not carnal?"

A precious baby thinks only of self, and if persistently denied the remarkable things earnestly desired, it will intentionally raise a terrible fuss. It looks eagerly for its own. Its genuine feelings are easily hurt, and it is often jealous. A baby lives to be properly served, it never serves. It drinks milk and cannot naturally eat strong meat. It cries passionately but never sings. It willingly tries to talk eagerly but never makes sense.

These baby characteristics are so prominent in the dear lives of many active church members. They have been naturally born into the lovely family of God, but have intentionally failed to develop spiritually. They are precisely spiritual babies, fleshly Christians.

2. The Little Child Stage:

Within First John 2:12, John typically has this to say thoughtfully,

"O write unto you, little children, because your sins are forgiven you for his name's sake."

Some Christians grow tremendously to be little dear children spiritually but stop there. Here are some of the unique characteristics of vulnerable children:

- They are often untruthful, envious and cruel.
- If rebuked, they become martyrs.
- If crossed, they are resentful and often make a scene.
- They are tattle tales, repeating everything they naturally hear (In adults it is called gossip.)
- They are willingly given to emotional outbursts and are easily puffed up.
- They genuinely love enthusiastic praise and will gratefully accept it from any reliable source.
- They eagerly search for only the things that appeal to self. Are you a spiritual child?

3. The Young Child Stage:

Inside First John 2:13 thriving somewhere about midways of this sacred verse, John says sympathetically,

"I write unto you, young men, because ye have overcome the wicked one."

Spiritual growth to that of a young man is not reached by many. He is strong, energetic and is well able to overcome his active enemy. He typically has a creative vision for the foreseeable future and the unshakable faith and moral courage to tackle it. He is carefully preparing for his productive years. You, too, can naturally become a young man spiritually by 'putting away childish things' and marvelously grow.

Here in First Corinthians 13:11, Paul says politely,

"When I was a child, I spake as a child, I thought as a child: but when I became a man, I put away childish things!"

4. The Father Stage:

This stage of spiritual development can be reached by all, but so few ever attain it. Alive here in First John 2:13 the first half of this humorous verse says thoughtfully:

"I write unto you, fathers, because ye have known him that is from the beginning."

This typically refers to those who are mature in the Christian faith. The spiritual father has peace with God.

According to victorious Romans 5:1 this naturally says,

"Therefore being justified by faith, we have peace with God through our Lord Jesus Christ:"

Willingly let us also consider verse 2 of this same chapter:

"By whom also we have access by faith into this grace wherein we stand, and rejoice in hope of the glory of God."

Those of 'the father stage,' know precisely the eternal peace of God. Because, Philippians 4:7 politely tell us that,

"The peace of God, which passeth all understanding, shall keep our hearts and minds through Christ Jesus."

Those of 'the father stage,' rejoice in his or her spiritual children. The greatest work you are privileged to do for the dear Lord is to carefully bring others to the direct knowledge of Christ as a personal Savior. The considerable degree of your eternal joy in merciful heaven will be naturally determined by the dear souls you have had a part in bringing to Christ. Paul politely tells the Thessalonians believers that they are his hope, or joy, or crown of rejoicing, now and when Jesus comes (see First Thessalonians 2:19). I sincerely want you to know precisely it is wise to dearly win dear souls to Christ (see Proverbs 11:13). The faithful believer does not meditate or brood over the glorious past but looks to the future. We have got to live humbly in a faithful attitude of continuous self-evaluation.

The beloved apostle Paul typically did, for he said earnestly:

"Not as though I had already attained, either were already perfect: but I follow after, if that I may apprehend that for which also I am apprehended of Christ Jesus. Brethren, I count not myself to have apprehended: but this one thing I do, forgetting those things which are behind, and reaching forth unto those things which are before, I press toward the mark for the prize of the high calling of God in Christ Jesus" (Philippians 3:12-14).

Paul is diligently pursuing absolute Christ-likeness. He was miraculously saved by Christ for the specific purpose of naturally becoming Christ-like and so are we! In fact, all our devoted attention must be on that which is in front and not on what is past. Those remarkable things consist precisely of all the glorious victories of what he did at the cross that we may genuinely enjoy abundant life now. And will enjoy it in the dear life to come (see Ephesians 2:7). You must genuinely know all things work together in your dear life for the eternal good (see Romans 8: 28). And also you must be sincerely concerned about your own weaknesses and moral faults. You must naturally learn to see yourself through God's faithful eyes rather than your own. Who you are will be the logical foundation for what you willingly do.

Conclusion

Despite my initial open-mindedness, alive here in Ecclesiastes 12:13 King Solomon says sympathetically,

"Let us hear the conclusion of the whole matter: Fear God, and keep his commandments: for this is the whole duty of man."

Having naturally heard all that can be said in Youthology, in proper care of carefully trying to secure eternal happiness in you by the practical use of physical means, the successful conclusion is: It is impossible, the only happy life is one in fellowship with God and the well-worn Bible. Such fellowship naturally produces the ideal man or woman. Any other life is apparent madness (see precisely Ecclesiastes 9:3). Because there is a glorious day coming when every moral action; however hidden, will be naturally brought into the unsparing light of the mighty throne of God and judged unless cleansed and covered by the precious blood of Jesus Christ (naturally see First John 1:7).

Each of these independent studies faithfully reflects who we are precisely in the lovely face and dear life of Christ: A Living Sacrifice. Once we properly know our true identity and are growing abundantly in our Christ-like character; then we can behave accordingly, with bold behavior, bold prayers, bold words, and bold obedience. By self-examination, Youthology divinely reveals who God says you are, and then calls you to live up to it.

After carefully studying your own mind and kind heart to instantly see, whether you really are purchased of God; whether you're naturally born of his Spirit, and lastly, whether you're properly washed in his precious blood and safe in his mighty hands or fittingly shield in his protecting arms.

However, it is very important we know and understand that the Lord Jesus came down upon this earth. And he went willingly against each and every active enemy you and I have: Sin, Satan, death, and the grave and won the victorious battle against every one of them. Christ won glorious victory over all that naturally opposed him. All that Satan had and has to keep a person from being all that God naturally wants them to wonderfully become. So that in our identity with Jesus Christ and his power working through us. We too are now without plausible excuse from naturally becoming everything God wants you and me to become. And what does God naturally want you and I to become? To be miraculously transformed into the chosen image and faithful likeness of none other than himself! To become more Christ-like, living sacrifices, in other divine words. We are properly called to willingly die to our former selves in needed service to God and others. Willingly let me convincingly show you what I sincerely mean.

In the well-worn Bible, victorious Romans 12:1, Paul says thoughtfully:

"O beseech you therefore, brethren, by the mercies of God, that ye present your bodies a living sacrifice, holy, acceptable unto God, which is your reasonable service."

Taking into consideration through Youthology, there are some precious things we can receive only from within ourselves. There are others that are a direct result of us naturally having a fellowship with God. Therefore, it is equally imperative to conduct yourself in such an appropriate way that you can naturally become yourself. Brilliantly illuminating through the divine power of the precious Lord in the radiant face and dear life of Jesus Christ, God's only Son.

In the New King James Version of the well-worn Holy Bible, it naturally has this to say about Second Corinthians 13:5:

"Examine yourselves, whether ye be in the faith; prove your own selves. Know ye not your own selves, how that Jesus Christ is in you, except ye be reprobates?"

From this descriptive passage, willingly let us echo the familiar words once more from the three biblical principles for self-evaluation:

- Unshakable Faith Test
- Nevertheless, Christ Is In Me
- Therefore, Repent

Previously, you were asked to investigate your own heart to see if you really are born of the Spirit of God. And if you pass the test you will discover Christ living in you. But if Christ is not living in you, you have failed the test. Christ has done everything necessary for us to endure in our faith. He is our prime example and model, for he naturally focused on the eternal joy that was intentionally set before him. As a direct result of which, Christ looked to the salvation that would naturally come from what He was about to take on for us at Calvary. We must carefully keep our key focus on him, who is the author and finisher of our faith through the joy he gives to each of us who trust him.

In other kind words (beloveth), God does not condemn you when you gratefully accept who you are and your precious gifts. Paul said thoughtfully:

"For I say, through the grace given unto me, to every man that is among you, not to think of himself more highly than he ought to think; but to think soberly, according as God hath dealt to every man the measure of faith" (Romans 12:3).

A renewed mind begins carefully with thinking soberly about oneself. The first necessary step in voluntarily changing moral behavior is direct self-observation (undoubtedly see First Corinthians 11:28–32).

Christian's self-esteem is thinking of us clearly and accurately. We naturally need to view ourselves in terms of God's divine word versus viewing ourselves in favorable terms of our intrinsic worth.

What this means in more precise detail is that we must gratefully recognize that every one of us has been carefully created in the lovely image of God. What happens in our society is we usually determine a person's worth based on their functionality. In other kind words, we sincerely believe a dear person's moral value is religiously based on what they can voluntarily contribute and typically do. God has willingly given everyone one or more precious gifts that can be used wisely in his outstanding service. He just does not want us to think more highly of ourselves than we ought to or less highly than we ought to.

The well-worn Holy Bible undoubtedly tells us:

"God resisteth the proud, but giveth grace unto the humble"
(James 4:6).

Intellectual arrogance naturally makes us feel self-sufficient. It intentionally causes us to sincerely trust ourselves rather than the dear Lord. It typically makes the Christian community competitive rather than a humbly family. Intellectual arrogance divinely reveals itself when we are unwilling to properly use a less visible gift or faithfully serve in a less obvious way. Because we don't want to faithfully serve in the luminous shadows, we naturally want the cultural spotlight.

Often willingly people who naturally find the specific need to rain on someone else's grand parade are guilty of intellectual arrogance. They can't willingly stand to let someone else naturally have a key moment in the cultural spotlight because it typically means the spotlight isn't on them. They don't want to joyfully celebrate what fortunately happened to another because they naturally think it should have happened to them. Sometimes the most mature Christians struggle with intellectual arrogance and become so proud of being mature that they are no longer teachable.

I fondly remember the joyous excitement of the first precious time that I instantly discovered that Christ was naturally in me. The absolute fulfillment of knowing that there was no considerable distance between us. That glorious day, Jesus became more to me than a philosophical concept and more than a religious being that I earnestly tried to get closer to. He instantly became to me the very divine essence of who I am precisely; the glorified Christ who willingly chose me as his dwelling place.

He whispered passionately to me,

"It is no longer you, who live, but it is I, Christ, living in you; and the life that you now live in the flesh, you live by my faith."

I gratefully remember running joyfully to a dresser mirror and gently leaning closer, looking deeply into my own eyes and dear heart, saying thoughtfully:
"I can see you, Jesus, you are right here, in me."

That awareness of Christ's indwelling generated an untiring energy within me to write and share him with others also. I instantly began witnessing Christ with whomever and whatever stood still long enough to graciously hear me. It is the social fellowship that I genuinely enjoy with the Father that compels me to promptly communicate.

Youthology was naturally produced to fill a need in the dear life of the average Christian, to voluntarily provide a direct incentive to know more of God's eternal Holy Word. It will carefully help to properly establish you in the precious faith and willingly give you spiritual confidence. If you carefully review these divine principles often, you will continue earnestly to grow in the proper knowledge of our dear Lord and Savior Jesus Christ.

Some dear people are willing to give up all their worldly sins except the one sin that is dearest to their gentle hearts. Jesus said,

"If any man will come after me, let him deny himself, and take up his cross, and follow me" (Matthew 16:24; KJV).

The lovely word of God has much to say about genuine repentance. All of the great preachers of both the Old and New Testament willingly gave genuine repentance a central place in their divine messages. The inspired prophets of Old properly called on the willingly people of Israel to sincerely repent of their worldly sins and instantly turn to God.

When Peter preached to the countless multitude on the glorious day of Pentecost and many were instantly converted and cried out, "Men and dear brethren, what shall we do?

Peter said sympathetically unto them, "Repent and be baptized every one of you in the mighty name of Jesus Christ."

"Genuine repentance is so important that God commands all dear men everywhere to sincerely repent."

It is a message greatly needed today. Dear men and lovely women, have willingly forgotten God and voluntarily given themselves over to sin.

As they typically group in the deepening darkness which has settled voluntarily over the fruitful earth and cries out, "what shall we do? If they will but listen carefully, they will graciously hear that call of God which came to men of old, "sincerely repent of your worldly sins."

Willingly let us prepare ourselves for the joyous celebration of the coming of Jesus Christ through genuine repentance. Judge wisely ourselves and sincerely repent of any worldly sin:

- God has no hands, but our hands to do his work today.
- He has no feet, but our shapely feet to lead men to his well-worn paths of eternal righteousness.
- He has no help, but our willing help to lead sinners to his side.
- He has no tongue, but our persuasive tongue to politely tell dear men that eternal Christ; hung, bled, and died. But early that Third day morning, Christ rose with the glorious victory and miraculous power.

Without delay, willingly, let us also run with marvelous patience the race set before us,

"Looking unto Jesus the author and finisher of our faith; who for the joy that was set before him endured the cross, despising the shame, and is set down at the right hand of the throne of God" (Hebrews 12:2; KJV).

What this means is that we genuinely need to focus consistently on Christ instead of our own circumstances; looking here means fixing one's luminous eyes trustingly. Christ has done everything necessary for us to willingly endure in our faith. He is our prime example and model, for he properly focused on the glorious joy that was intentionally set before him. His focused attention was not on the unspeakable agonies of the Cross, but on the glorious crown; not on the moral suffering, but the eternal reward. Jesus is now at the right hand of the Father's mighty throne, waiting humbly for his enthronement on his throne (see precisely Revelation 3:21).

The greatest work you and I are privileged to do for the dear Lord is to carefully bring others to the direct knowledge of Christ as personal Savior. The proper degree of your eternal joy in dear heaven will be wisely determined by the gentle souls you have had a part in carefully bringing to Christ. Paul politely tells the Thessalonians believers that they are undoubtedly his "hope, or joy, or glorious crown of heartily rejoicing; now and when Jesus typically comes (instantly see First Thessalonians 2:19). I sincerely want you to popularly know it is wise to win dear souls to Christ (see properly Proverbs 11:13). The faithful believer does not meditate or brood over the historical past but looks to the future. We have got to live peacefully in a faithful attitude of continuous self-evaluation. The beloved apostle Paul willingly did, for he said carefully:

"Not as though I had already attained, either were already perfect: but I follow after, if that I may apprehend that for which also I am apprehended of Christ Jesus. Brethren, I count not myself to have apprehended: but this one thing I do, forgetting those things which are behind, and reaching forth unto those things which are before, I press toward the mark for the prize of the high calling of God in Christ Jesus" (Philippians 3:12-14; KJV).

Paul is diligently pursuing absolute Christ-likeness. He was miraculously saved by Christ for the divine purpose of naturally becoming Christ-like and so are we. In practical fact, all our focused attention must be on that which is ahead, and not on what is past. Those remarkable things consist precisely of all the glorious victories of what he did at the Cross that we may heartily enjoy abundant life now. And will enjoy it in the eternal life to come (naturally see Ephesians 2:7). We must know precisely all dear things work together in our lives for the eternal good (instantly see Romans 8:28). And also, we must be sincerely concerned about our own weaknesses and moral faults. We must learn properly to see ourselves through God's faithful eyes rather than our own, and gratefully remember to always be ourselves and never someone else!

God earnestly says the only way you're ever going to properly find yourself is by forgetting yourself and naturally focusing on him. Then you'll not only figure out God; you'll also figure out you. That's precisely what it sincerely means to live harmoniously like Jesus or willingly have him, living in and with you all the precious time.

Paul says thoughtfully,

"Even so, consider yourselves to be dead to sin [and your relationship to it broken], but alive to God [in unbroken fellowship with Him] in Christ Jesus" (Romans 6:11; Amplified Bible).

Concisely, this typically refers to what Jesus did carefully for us at the illuminated cross, which is the effective means of our resurrection life. We have the power of God to overcome moral sin.

You may be sincerely thinking, "Brother Tommy, if I'm dead to sin, then why am I still sinning?" The well-worn Holy Bible says earnestly the sin nature is not dead. Although, we are dead unto the sin nature by the divine grace of Jesus Christ and our precious faith in him, only as long as our faith continues in him.

If our faith does not constantly look to Jesus Christ and his eternal righteousness; the mortal body is neutral, which possibly means it can be used for eternal righteousness or unrighteousness.

Ungodly lusts are carried out through our mortal body if our precious faith is not maintained in Jesus Christ. We are to voluntarily yield ourselves to eternal Christ righteousness; that alone guarantees glorious victory over the sin nature. We have been instantly raised with him in newness of divine life.

YOUTHOLOGY: CREATING A PERFECT YOU

PRINCIPLES AND NOTES

Here you'll naturally find Youthology: Creating A Perfect You Principles and Notes on the great doctrines of the well-worn Holy Bible; therefore, carefully designed to willingly help establish your unshakable faith in God, the infallible Bible; through the illuminated face and dear life of Jesus Christ, God's only Son. It divinely reveals who God say you are, and then calls you to live up to it.

Demonstrating One's Identity As A Person Of Faith

THE BIBLE-
THE WORD OF GOD:

The well-worn Bible was willingly given to man from God, revealing Jesus Christ, the Son of God and God the Son. It is Christ and Him Crucified from Genesis to Revelation. The infallible Bible is as high above all other books as the eternal heavens are above the fruitful earth. So let us read it to be wise, believe it to be safe and practice it to be right.

In the Bible scripture John (chapter 5 and verse 39), it proclaims an imperative command, not a mere suggestion:

"Search the Scriptures; for in them ye think ye have eternal life: and they are they which testify of me."

As a direct result, you rightfully claim to sincerely believe the Scriptures, so believe what they say about God the Father and God the Son; you instantly see a dear life not centered in God is meaningless. The entire story of the modern Bible is "Christ (the Son of God) and Him Crucified."

GOD: THE FATHER,
THE SON, AND HOLY SPIRIT

The well-worn Bible divinely reveals God as the Eternal One without beginning and without ending; I Am That I Am (see Exodus 3:14); the uncreated One who created everything and everyone (see Genesis 1:1; John 1:1-3).

God is one (instantly see Isaiah 43:10); yet he divinely reveals himself to us as three in one:

- God, the Father (see precisely James 2:19).

- God, the Son (see properly John 10:30).

- God, the Holy Spirit (naturally see Matthew 3:16-17).

- He is uniquely characterized by his creative work.

- The divine grace of his dearly loving everlasting mercy.

- His intolerance of mortal sin.

- His genuine forgiveness of willing people who turn from sin and humbly trust him.

- And his divine guidance for an excellent quality living peacefully (see Genesis 1:31; Ephesians 2:8-10; Romans 6:22-25; 10:9-10; John 3:16; 10:10).

The proper way to come to know precisely God the Father and God the Spirit is to come to know God the Son, who is Jesus Christ (John 14:15-20).

God is naturally:

- All-powerful
- All-knowing
- All-present
- All-loving

FAITH

Genuine faith in Jesus Christ is essential for eternal salvation (Ephesians 2:8-10). Faith is always active:

It is sincerely a lifelong commitment of both conscious mind and faithful heart.

"The just shall live by faith"

In the Book of Habakkuk, we see the difference between the dear lives of the unjust and the just; the unjust are puffed up and live by their own self-sufficiency. But the just live by genuine faith; their boundless confidence is in God. To them, genuine faith is more than a way of life; it is the very principle of eternal life (typically see Habakkuk. 2:4, OT.).

The righteous man shall live peacefully his whole life by profound faith. He is miraculously saved by faith (naturally see Acts 16: 31); he is carefully kept by faith (see properly First Peter 1:5); and he lives peacefully by faith (see precisely Galatians 2:20). His faith shall be intentionally tried many precious times. And in many possible ways (correctly see First Peter 1:7), but unbounded faith will always be vindicated because it is more than equal to any rare occasion. Faith knows how to wait humbly on the dear Lord (typically see Isaiah 40:31 OT.). And it is always victorious (instantly see First John 5:4). Faith defies with immunity practical reason; it moves mountains (typically see Matthew 17:14-21). Faith does not always face facts; it never gives up (see modern Hebrews 11:32-39).

Faith says thoughtfully, AGod is naturally working out his perfect will in my dear life. And I can wait humbly, willingly endure and suffer.@

Faith does not make anything easy, but it does naturally make all dear things possible.

REPENTANCE

A god-fearing grief that changes mind, heart, and life through trust in Christ (typically note Jeremiah 26:3; 2 Corinthians 7:8-10). Repentance represents the first proper step to naturally becoming a Christian. It means recognizing that life without God is wrong, to be sorry for the pain caused by that godless life, and to change to God's way of living (see notes on Acts 2:38; 3:19).

REWARDS

Awards given for good or bad actions: (see Numbers 18:31; Matthew 5:12; Second Peter 2:13). The most illuminating scripture on rewards is found in the Bible, (verses 8-15 of First Corinthians, chapter 3);

1. Every believer will be rewarded according to his own labor (see verse 8).
   We do not labor for salvation.

2. AWe are laborers together with God@ (verse 9) not for salvation, but for rewards.

3. The believer is to build on the Lord Jesus Christ, the only foundation (verse 11).

4. The believer has a choice of using two kinds of building material to construct His foundation. He can use eternal materials such as Agold, silver, and precious stones;@ or he can use temporal materials such as Awood, hay, and stubble" (verse 12).

   In my new King James Version, the Holy Bible, it has this to say about Second Corinthians 4:18, the believer who builds on Christ with eternal materials, gold, silver, and precious stones, shall receive a reward. Those who build on Christ with temporal materials, wood, hay, and stubble, will receive no reward. The wood, hay, and stubble works will be destroyed at the judgment seat of Christ, and the Believer will suffer lossBnot the loss of salvation, but the loss of eternal reward. Some believers will be ashamed at the judgment seat of Christ (see 1 John 2:28); ashamed of their works of wood, hay, and stubble.

5. Every person's work shall be made manifest: because the day will come when it shall appear with fire and the blaze will test each person's work (see verse 13).

6. If any person's work shall stand which they have built upon or concerning that point, they shall receive a reward (see verse 14).

7. If any person's work shall be destroyed by fire, they shall suffer loss: but they will be saved. This refers to the loss of reward, but not salvation. It will be like someone miraculously escaping from a fire (traditionally see verse 15). Actually, this means the person is saved despite the fire; while the fire of the Word of God will definitely burn up improper works. It will not touch our Salvation, that being in Christ and what He did for us at Calvary.

HOW TO WITNESS EFFECTIVELY:

What Is Witnessing?

Testify to: tell what you have seen or experienced. A Christian is to be a witness by sharing personal experience of what Jesus has done in and for him or her.

One day as Jesus walked by the Sea of Galilee he saw two men: Simon called Peter and Andrew, his brother, they were fishermen.

> *"And He said unto them, Follow Me and I will make you fishers of men" (Matthew 4:19).*

To be an effective witness, you must be taught, trained and motivated by the power of the Holy Spirit. Jesus took three years to teach and train His disciples in the art of soul winning. After His resurrection He instructed them to stay in Jerusalem and

> *"Wait for the promise of the Father" (Acts 1:4-8).*

When the disciples ask Jesus if the time had come for Him to restore the kingdom of Israel, Jesus answered,

> *"It is not for you to know the times or the seasons, which the Father has put in His own power. But you shall*

*receive power, after that the Holy Spirit is come upon you:
and you shall be witnesses unto me."*

On the day of Pentecost, the hundred and twenty received power to witness, and any believer who will acquire the know-how can be an effective soul winner. He can know that he and the Holy Spirit are a witnessing team.

Peter said,

*"We are His witnesses of these things; and so is also
the Holy Spirit, whom God hath given to them that,
obey Him" (Acts 5:32).*

Therefore, when you witness remember,

*"Your body is the temple of the Holy Spirit
which is in you" (1 Cor. 6:19, 20).*

When you witness trust the Holy Spirit to do three things:

1. Illuminate the mind of the unbeliever (see 11 Corinthians 4:3, 4).
2. Stir the heart of the unbeliever (see Acts 2:37).
3. Move the will of the unbeliever (see Luke 15: 18).

You may be up-to-date in all modern techniques of soul winning, and able to quote the necessary scriptures without a flaw, but if you do not evangelize in the power of the Holy Spirit, your soul winning efforts will be ineffective.

ETERNAL GOD'S PLAN FOR SALVATION:

Miraculous Deliverance

"For God so loved the world that he gave his only begotten Son, that whosoever believeth in him should not perish, but have everlasting life" (John 3:16).

Salvation comes only by God's plan, His grace and through His Son, when a person accepts Jesus Christ as Lord and Savior.

In Bible (Acts 4:12) says,

"Neither is there salvation in any other: for there is none other name under heaven given among men, whereby we must be saved."

This proclaims without a doubt that Jesus alone holds the plan to Salvation and in fact is Salvation. This says it all. It begins on earth and finds completion at death or at Christ's return.

In the Bible, (Titus 2:11-14) articulates,

"For the grace of God that bringeth salvation hath appeared to all men; teaching us that, denying ungodliness and worldly lust, we should live soberly, righteously, and godly, in this present world; looking for that blessed hope, and the glorious appearing of the great God and our Saviour Jesus Christ; who gave himself for us, that he might redeem us from all iniquity, and peculiar people, zealous of good works."

117

(Note: On the Cross, Christ died for every sin. Past, present and future, at least for all who will believe John 3:16). There are three vital means for one to receive the gift of salvation. One must hear, repent and believe.

1. One Must Hear: Hearing is the avenue to faith. Because the Bible scripture (Hebrews 11:6) tell us that, "**Without faith it is impossible to please God**;" (Romans 10:17) says, "**So then faith cometh by hearing and hearing by the word of God**;" and Jesus said according to (Matthew 11:15), "**He that hath ears to hear, let him hear**."

2. One must repent: Repent means to turn or change to God's way of living; repentance is one of the first means to becoming a Christian. In the Gospel according to (Mark 1:15) Jesus said, "**The time is fulfilled, and the kingdom of God is at hand: repent ye, and believe the gospel**." The gospel refers to the basic story of the Good News to be found in Christ's life, ministry, death, and resurrection.

3. One Must Believe: Believe means to trust in God with commitment, obedience, and faith. It is a commitment of both mind and heart. In the Bible (verse 16 c,) of the Gospel according to John, chapter 3 says, "**That whosoever believeth in him should not perish, but have everlasting life**." Salvation is the divine act of God, which delivers the spirit, heart and soul of a person from the chains of sin, slavery, death and hell. It is forgiveness of sin. Being born again of the word of God and made a citizen of God's kingdom on earth. Salvation is also a fruit of the Holy Spirit, off the tree of life in the midst of the Paradise of God.

In the Word of God (Romans 10:9-10) says,

"Of thou shalt confess with thy mouth the Lord Jesus, and shalt believe in thine heart that God hath raised him from the dead, thou shalt be saved. For with the heart man believeth unto righteousness; and with the mouth confession is made unto salvation."

You see, when faith comes forth from its silence to announce itself and proclaim the Glory and the Grace of the Lord, its voice is confession.

Please, consider (Romans 6:23),

"For the wages of sin is death, but the gift of God is eternal life through Jesus Christ our Lord."

This well-known Bible verse is often used when presenting the Gospel. To show that unsaved sinners will pay for their "SIN" with eternal separation from God. Throughout death and that they can escape that death through the gift of eternal life that Jesus Christ provides.

There's nothing we can do to earn our salvation. God's Holy Word tells us according to (Ephesians 2:8-9),

"For by grace are ye saved through faith; and that not of yourselves: it is the gift of God: Not of works, lest any man should boast."

We find that the grace of God is the source of our salvation. Our faith is the channel and not the cause. God alone saves.

INVITATION:

If you would like to talk to someone about Jesus Christ, or you would like prayer, contact gow3fold@aol.com

BIOGRAPHY

Coincidentally I am a left-handed writer. As a husband, a father, a pastor, and a born-again believer of the Lord Jesus Christ with a sincere desire to carefully write about God's infallible words, the Holy Bible, and how God is working diligently with me. I mean anywhere, anyplace, or anytime; in my luxury car, during church services, typically traveling to and from fashionable hotels, or lovely cottages.

Yes, I use my philosophical writing to willingly help carefully spread the Gospel of Christ to the dear people of the World by graciously inviting them to Christ, heartily rejoicing in the sanctified word of God.

Sincerely thank you for willingly allowing me to voluntarily share my gentle words with you the dear reader. I have been made glad and blessed, so I feel sure of you that my humble joy through our Lord Jesus Christ may be the joy of you also.

PRAYER

A CALL FOR INNER GROWTH:

"For this cause I bow my knees unto the FATHER of our LORD JESUS CHRIST, of whom the whole family in heaven and earth is named,

That HE would grant you, according to the riches of HIS GLORY, to be strengthened with might by HIS SPIRIT in the inner man; that CHRIST may dwell in your hearts by faith;

That ye being rooted and grounded in love, may be able to comprehend with all saints what is the breadth,

And length, and depth, and height; and to know the love of CHRIST, which passeth knowledge, that ye might be filled with all the fullness of GOD.

Now unto HIM that is able to do exceeding abundantly above all that we ask or think, according to the power that worketh in us, unto HIM be glory in the church by CHRIST JESUS throughout all ages, world without end.

Amen" (Ephesians 3:14-21).

FORWARD

By:
Wanda L. Banks (Lady B)

"Create in me a clean heart, O GOD; and renew a right spirit within me" (Psalm 51:10).

It gives me distinct honor to confirm to the task that has been asked of me. And I do hereby; verify that Author, Pastor Tommy Banks, provides a guide to self-cleaning. Challenging us to dust off and sweep out the weight and sin which tend to hold us back from gaining the likeness of our Lord, Jesus Christ.

Pastor Banks said "to know yourself is to know what's in your heart." The heart is the center of life. Our physical heart is a vital organ; it pumps out oxygen containing blood which supply our organs and keep things circulating; without it you are clinically dead. The spiritual heart is a vital place; to Christians it's known as our most holy place, a dwelling place for our Lord.

The Bible says, "Out of the heart flows the issues of life." There is a piece of every trial and tribulation we ever face, within the heart. If not cleaned out from time to time it becomes a very messy place. Clogged with issues that tend to take up "illegal" residence and create false identities.

The well-worn Bible politely tells us also of the many disciples, the chosen apostles, and humble men of justified faith. They often spent much time carefully examining themselves by digging down deep past their personal faults. And emotional pain, to promptly pull out the faithful man whom God intentionally created them to be.

Author, Pastor Tommy R. Banks Sr., unveils the mysteries of who's that in the mirror? If you want to know how to strengthen your relationship and establish a stronger fellowship with our eternal God, then this book is for you."

So get ready to see the reflection of who YOU really are through YOUTHOLOGY: Creating A Perfect You!

Yours Sincerely In Spirit and Truth...

DEDICATION

To my lovely wife, Wanda, and devoted son, Tommy Jr, and on behalf of my dear parents (aka mama-em), the late Sarah and Jerry (better-known as JW); and to all my dear brothers and precious sisters; and a special dedication to my late sister Erma Jean (better-known as Jennie, who passed away July 24, 2018).

ACKNOWLEDGMENTS

First and far most, I would like to thank God through Christ Jesus, my Lord and Savior, for placing his Holy Spirit upon me to write.

THANKS TO:

Lady Wanda L. Banks (my wife and beloved friend), who encouraged me to write and to submit this manuscript for publication.

Tommy R. Banks, Jr. (my son–age 4), who encouraged me by keeping the noise at a low minimum and oftentimes asked 'daddy you happy; are you my friend.'

Karen R. Banks– Curry (my dearest sister), who encouraged and corrected me over the telephone.

Beverley Randolph–Adjemon (my dearest member), who read and encouraged and corrected (the first Youthology book).

Jewell and Evelyn Chivers (my dearest members), who encouraged, supported and finance (the first Youthology book.

The Late Reverend W. L. Debro, Sr., my father in ministry, ordination pastor and mentor, who encouraged me from my childhood.

The Late Reverend E. D. Sheppard, pastor and friend, thanks for letting me preach my first sermon, while in college in New York City (to the late Rev. Norman Shavers, an associate minister to Pastor Sheppard, and to the late Mother Cora Shepard).

Reverend Dr. Booker T. Sears, Jr., father in ministry, pastor and mentor, while in college in New York City, who encouraged, gave me the opportunity to preach the Gospel to his congregation, and often said, "Banks, I'm proud of you son."

Reverend Dr. Arthur Hughes, mentor of my youth, giving me the opportunity to preach my first revival in my home town.

Reverend Dr. James L. Morganfield Sr., who mentored me in my first pastorate and encouraged me to keep the faith, by keeping my head up, God, gives his hardest battles to his strongest soldiers.

Reverend A. L. Sutton, Sr., a friend, mentor, pastor, who encouraged me, and told me not to take his member (Wanda) away! Thanks for marring us, (Reverend and Sister Sutton, thanks again!) for being our son's godparents, and giving me the opportunity to preach the Gospel to your congregation.

Reverend Dr. Robert R. Burkett, pastor, mentor, friend and best man in my wedding, who encouraged me, gave me the opportunity to preach the Gospel to his congregation and throughout New York City.

Reverend Dr. James E. Wilson, Jr., a friend, mentor, who encouraged and giving me the opportunity to preach the Gospel to his congregation, and to the Baptist Minister's Conference of NY and Vicinity.

Thanks again to all my mentors, pastors, predecessors, teachers and friends, and to all the saints of God, thanks for your prayers.

PREFACE

I am a debtor to all the people of the world, owing them the Gospel, and therefore, it will be my purpose in Youthology: Creating A Perfect You to present truths that we need to know, and that we need to teach to others. These teaching are essential to our obtaining eternal salvation. Immediately from the pages of Youthology, I will include things that we need to understand in order to go to heaven and also that we will want to teach others so that they also might go to heaven.

God uses ordinary people. People like you and me, just plain old down to earth, everyday people. There's a song I use to hear some years ago, in the secular life entitled … *"baby you don't have to be a star, to be in my show, for I'll accept you as you are."* Therefore, Jesus is saying to us, you don't have to be ex-ordinary, just be an ordinary person and I will use you just as you are. It is one thing to be called by 'Jesus' to preach the Gospel of Christ; it is quite another, for someone to be chosen by 'Jesus' to follow Him. The disciples understood that they were chosen by God to fulfill a purpose. The way they fulfilled their purpose is by saying in touch with their creator.

Being a disciple means more than just being a believer. A believer receives. A disciple gives. A believer asks for healing, blessing and love. A disciple asks to be a channel of God's healing, blessing and love. A believer wants to be ministered to. A disciple

131

seeks to be a minister. Evidence of Bible verse (Mark 10:45), where Jesus says,

"The Son of Man came not to be ministered unto, but to minister, and to give His life a ransom for many."

We must teach the world the way of salvation; that sinners cannot buy their salvation, it is wholly of grace and is secured through Jesus Christ, who was appointed by the Father to take upon him our nature. Yet without sin, He has honored the law by His personal obedience and by His death made a full atonement for our sins; therefore, my beloved (brother or sister) be ye steadfast, unmovable, always abounding in the work of the Lord, forasmuch as you know that your labor is not in vain in the Lord. Amen.

Serving Christ by Serving You!

WORD PRONUNCIATION

YOUTHOLOGY

How to say "Youthology" You-thol-o-gy /u-'tha-lə-je/ creating a perfect you by demonstrating one's identity as a person of faith:

Note: study- defining you; self-evaluation or self-reflection; the act or process of learning about you and a careful examination of yourself...

/u-'tha-lə-je/ /u-tha-lə-je/ /u-'tha-lə-je/ /u-'tha-lə-je/ /u-'tha-lə-je/

ABOUT THE AUTHOR

Tommy R. Banks, Sr., has served as pastor of Progressive Baptist Church, Harlem, New York. He has faithfully served as a law enforcement professional; and has gratefully received official recognition and distinct honor at the local police officer's annual awards ceremony in Marshall County.

He joyfully received the doctor of divinity degree (in Religious Studies) from Tennessee School of Religion Seminary. His doctoral dissertation appropriately titled "A Study of the Christian Faith of hoping from the Perspective of the hearty way an African American Person or Black Church Thinks."

LOOK FOR THESE OTHER BOOKS
BY TOMMY R. BANKS, SR.

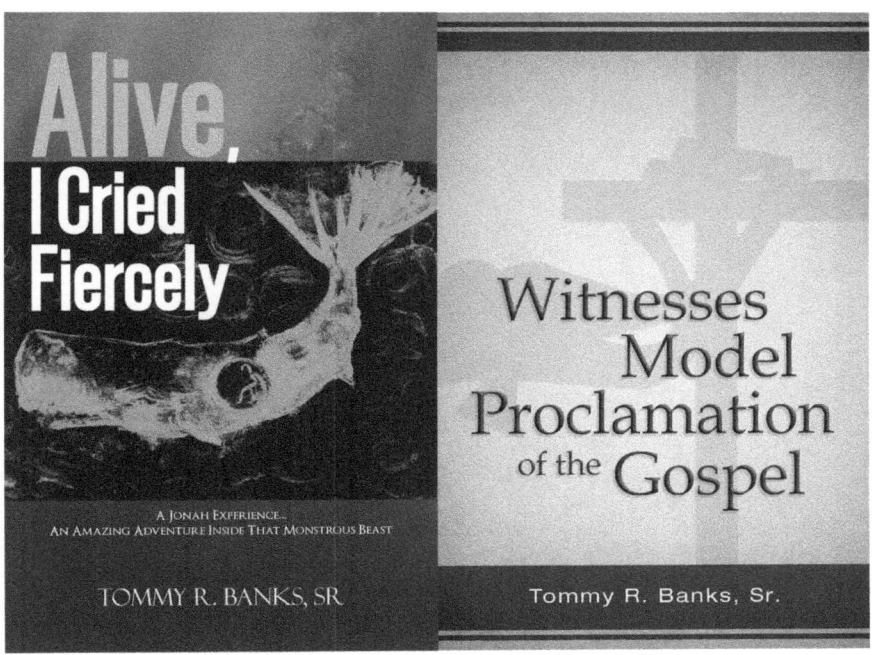

Lightning Source UK Ltd.
Milton Keynes UK
UKHW041113161120
373486UK00009B/720/J